A Practical Guide to French Business

A Practical Guide to French Business

Jon P. Alston
Melanie Hawthorne
and
Sylvie Saillet

Writers Club Press
New York Lincoln Shanghai

A Practical Guide to French Business

Writers Club Press
an imprint of iUniverse, Inc.

For information address:
iUniverse, Inc.
2021 Pine Lake Road, Suite 100
Lincoln, NE 68512
www.iuniverse.com

ISBN: 0-595-26462-X

Printed in the United States of America

To Kerry Cooper, who, as director of the international Business Programs, and Julian Gaspar, Director of the Center for International Studies, have been and continue to be major forces in the globalization of Texas A&M University.

To my French and American families, the Refoulés, Auberts, Alstons, Thomases, and my wife, Letitia, and to my good friend and colleague, Syed Tariq Anwar.

To my nephews Alistair and Laurence, with the hope that they have inherited the Francophile gene.

A mes parents, Joséphine et Michel, et à ma soeur Elisabeth, qui m'ont donné la chance d'étudier en France et aux Etats-Unis et permis de ce fait de participer 'a l'écriture de ce livre. Je remercie également Jon Alston, Texas A&M University et l'Ecole Supérieure de Commerce de Dijon.

Contents

INTRODUCTION

We have written this book describing the French style of business because knowledge of French business customs is necessary for those who expect to do business with French individuals. Since France has the world's fourth largest GNP and a population of 58,804,000, international businesspeople dare not ignore its economy. Yet when dealing with the French, ignorance of French business customs almost guarantees failure. Edward T. Hall and Mildred Reed Hall, leading international human resource consultants, state categorically (Hall and Hall, 1990: 120-1):

> Once you have decided to do business in France or with the French in the U.S., a strong commitment to do things the French way should accompany this decision. If there are chronic complaints from the Americans in France, the chances are that the Americans involved are not properly informed about how the French operate. It is essential to recruit employees who do not find French procedures, social customs, and savoir vivre stressful.

Unlike the Japanese, the French resist doing business "the American way." The French are proud of being unique and they expect foreigners to conform to their business protocols. The French attitude is that they are more intelligent and cultured than other nationalities, and that there is little need to adapt to others' business customs. Whenever they have a choice, French businesspersons select business partners who conform to their ways of doing business. In France, conforming to French business customs facilitates success. The French are very loyal and generous toward those they trust and respect. Respect is achieved by knowing how to act in ways the French recognize and accept.

The necessity of respecting French sensibilities is reflected in advertising content by McDonald's Corporation in France. In one ad placed in French magazines, a frowning cowboy in front of a US American flag says in French, "What I don't like about McDonald's in France is that they DON'T BUY American beef." The caption continues, "It's true John [his name is John in the ad], our meat does not come by cargo planes from the States. All of the meat used at McDonald's France comes from French cattle...and do you know why John? Because beef is as good here.... Anyway, nice hat John." McDonald's France has learned to be as French as possible; being seen as American by the French is counterproductive.

The French way of business is complex and difficult for foreigners to understand, in large part because the French are paradoxical; every statement describing a French business-related behavior is countered by its equally valid opposite. A French writer once noted that the French "were both cold blooded and passionate." He did not, however, explain how these paradoxes translated into day-to-day business behavior. That is why we have presented in this book specific protocols and French business behavior as well as general principles.

This cultural complexity is illustrated by the high levels of individualism found in French political thought and activity. Government officials are authoritarian and a common topic of discussion among the French is that "they," meaning bureaucrats, have too much power. The French want a government that regulates the social order but they are also famous for their attempts to avoid paying taxes and their acceptance of government controls. They understand that a national body with the national interest in mind is necessary while French individuals are willing to ignore whatever government direction they personally don't like.

French business has many rules and regulations; foreigners would say that red tape is a way of life in France and cannot be avoided. State officials watch over citizens by administering every detail of daily and business life. But the French also like to express their individuality by bending the rules and, especially, by resisting official demands when they are not to their advantage. Former President of France Charles de Gaulle once said that it was difficult to govern a land with 246 different kinds of cheese. He meant that governing the then fifty million individualists was a difficult and thankless task.

In spite of France's cultural complexity, there are strong tendencies that make generalizations possible. Despite their love of philosophy, the French are highly intolerant of ambiguity in daily affairs as measured by their level of uncertainty avoidance. Uncertainty avoidance is defined as a need for predictability in life, which often results in a need for many rules. Geert Hofstede (1980: 112) has measured the levels of uncertainty avoidance for fifty countries. Below are the uncertainty scores for selected countries. A higher score means a higher preference for certainty and hence for well-established rules:

France	**86**	Holland	53
Spain	86	**USA**	**46**
Italy	75	England	35
W. Germany	65	Sweden	29
Switzerland	59	Denmark	23

Strong uncertainty avoidance cultures, of which France is clearly one, contain certain recurring features. André Laurent found that managers in such countries (Laurent, 1983) believed that:

- organizational conflict hurts efficiency

- managers needed to know more than their subordinates

- detailed job descriptions were necessary to avoid confusion

- workers needed detailed and clear instructions to do their work well

There are also additional characteristics of high uncertainty avoidance cultures including the following beliefs:

- what is different, is dangerous; new ideas are suspect
- a rule that is ineffective is better than no rule
- emotions may be expressed at appropriate times
- precision is encouraged
- people should accept extensive guidance from their employers and government

The two sets of values listed above reflect French attitudes. This book explains these values so that those dealing with French businesspersons can understand French behavior patterns well enough (1) to avoid confusion and culture shock, and also (2) to be able to develop strategies that use these values to the reader's advantage.

Foreigners' confusion when dealing with the French derives not from the French propensity for rules, of which there are many. For the French are also individualists, and see rules as to be avoided or circumvented whenever doing so is to their benefit. Often, rules exist but French officials do not enforce them as rigidly as they might or else nothing would get done. The trick for foreigners, then, is to be able to know how to convince a French businessperson or government official that a rule should be enforced leniently.

French business attitudes and cultures are very different from those found elsewhere. Foreigners flock to France as tourists to enjoy its museums, eat its food, and experience both its urban life and countryside. By contrast, foreigners who come to France to do business often dislike their day-to-day dealings with the French, and US American businesspersons enjoy dealing with Germans and British businesspersons more than with their French counterparts. Other nationals complain about French behavior, too, and believe that the French are the most difficult nationality in terms of business. Japanese doing business in France also experience culture shock because of French complexity (Agence France Presse, 1991):

> Paris is hell for the Japanese. It gives them what one Japanese psychiatrist described as the "Paris Syndrome," which includes hallucinations, depression, paranoia and shocks to the nervous system.
>
> "French people tend to be moody," said Hiroaki Ota..."They can be very kind one moment and very mean the next." Mr. Ota treats fellow Japanese in Europe who are suffering from culture shock.
>
> "Japanese are shocked by these kinds of attitude changes as they are used to more predictable people in their native country," he said.

Hiroaki Ota treats some of the 25,000 Japanese living in Paris. Ota finds that Japanese at times react negatively to the emotionality of the French and that Japanese pragmatism conflicts with the French fascination with general principles and florid discussions. All foreigners who do not embrace French contradictions and use them to their advantage are likely to be both confused and ineffective.

Another source of confusion is the fact that French businesses differ not only from corporations from other societies, but also from one another. Peugeot has a different corporate culture from Elf Aquitaine. French newspapers have published articles on the "culture shock" when one French company merges with another as companies increasingly adopt the once rare practice in France of mergers and acquisitions.

Having pointed out some of the unique features of French culture (more are presented throughout this book), let us note that the French are not completely different from other nationalities and it is possible to understand why they behave as they do. The similar values are often expressed in unique ways, and the priorities of certain values differ, but the French can be understood. Those who understand how and why the French behave the way they do find great satisfaction when interacting with the French.

Below are the responses of business executives to questions about the rankings of their general values. Each value comes with emotional baggage and meanings unique to each national culture. For example, the term "equality" for US Americans includes the notion of fairness; people may not necessarily be equal, but they should have the *opportunity* to be equal through their own efforts. The French, on the other hand, assume people are different from one another and may have different goals and interests. They should be allowed to seek these goals by being self-reliant. Thus, US Americans and French define the values of "equality" and "self-reliance" very differently, and, as the list below indicates, each national sample gives different ranks:

PRIORITY OF VALUES

US AMERICAN	FRENCH
1. Equality	1. Self-reliance
2. Freedom	2. Freedom
3. Openness	3. Openness
4. Self-reliance	4. Relationships
5. Cooperation	5. Time
6. Family Security	6. Spirituality
7. Relationships	7. Materialism
8. Privacy	8. Equality
9. Group Harmony	9. Competition
10. Time	10. Group harmony

Source: Adapted from Elashmawi and Harris (1993): 58 and 61.

This book serves to make French business-related attitudes and patterns more understandable to non-French. Knowledge of at times contradictory French mindsets and business habits makes dealing with the French less mysterious and less frustrating.

The interaction of French and US American businesspersons is made more difficult by the fact that each group holds negative stereotypes of the other. While national stereotypes usually have a core of truth to them, stereotypes can also mislead. Stereotypes can offer hints of true national character although reality is always more complex than such preconceived biases. According to multi-cultural experts Alfons Trompenaars and Charles Hampden-Turner (1998: 25), French and US Americans hold the following stereotypes about each other:

Americans view French as:	French view Americans as:
Arrogant	Naive
Flamboyant	Aggressive
Hierarchical	Unprincipled
Emotional	Workaholic

While these generalizations are partly true, these stereotypes ignore the fact that both French and US Americans vary with regard to the above attributes. There are many French workaholics and there are many US Americans who are less dedicated to their work. In fact, there are distinct differences among working French by age, occupation, and region of residence. Younger French non-manual workers are more "Americanized" than their older colleagues and are more comfortable (or at least understand) American business practices. Many speak English and have lived and studied in the United States. French executives in fact work long hours, though they consider it bad taste to mention this fact. Southern French, reflecting a more Latin or Mediterranean stereotype, are considered to be less work-oriented and more emotionally expressive than French from the North or Paris, who conform more to the repressed or Protestant work ethic stereotype more common in Anglo Saxon cultures. Parisians are seen by other

French as rude, too commercial and interested solely in profit, and too interested in work. For their part, Parisians see non-Parisians as unsophisticated and more traditional.

Franco-American interaction today is made more difficult by the fact that, in the 1990s, US Americans have regained their traditional optimism and brashness that many had lost during the Vietnamese War and the Japanese control of many local markets during the 1970s and 1980s. Americans once again have very positive feelings about themselves and their culture. Non-US Americans, including the French, see this attitude as cultural arrogance.

The French resent the implications that their culture is inferior to that of the United States. Richard D. Lewis, in his discussion of national blind spots, points to the French insistence that "the length and magnificence of their historical achievement simply leave them convinced that they have a mission to teach and civilize others...." and that "[t]heir political, military, and economic strengths no longer predominate as they once did, but the French perceive no diminishment or fading of their moral and didactic authority" (Lewis, 2003: 122). The French feel superior to others and resent being told how to behave.

By the same token, the French, especially French intellectuals, exhibit a sense of uncertainty about the viability (much less the superiority) of their culture and society. Many French, and foreign observers, believe that French society is in a crisis. The reader who glances at the references, the Suggested Readings in this book, and at the general literature on various aspects of French society will note the many titles that reflect doubt about the health of French society:

The Stalled Society.	*The Crisis of the Cadres.*
France on the Brink.	*France in Crisis.*
The French Disease.	*The Present Crisis.*
L'Elysée in Danger.	*Crisis and Decline.*

A typical criticism of French society is that its leaders refuse to face reality and prefer to maintain the traditional patterns of social structures that give them power and prestige. One of France's most famous sociologists, Michel Crozier, made this observation of French society and business practices (Crozier, 1973: 60-1):

> In the case of France, the social system is stuck fast in a system of partitions and barriers, of secrecy and irresponsibility, so that difficult decisions are fudged and each individual is assured the system's general protection from all sanctions—even that of publicity. Groups, categories, and even individuals refuse to confront one another directly. The protective shadow of secrecy, complexity, and state intervention is needed to solve a problem or sweep it under the carpet.

This book provides the reader with the knowledge to deal successfully, and with a minimum of frustration, with the "shadows" Crozier feels inhibit France's full entry into the modern world.

This sense of cultural crisis that is held by many French people creates feelings of insecurity and anger when French deal with US Americans. It is very easy for even those US Americans with the best intentions to irritate French businesspersons and create conflict. These feelings are often counterproductive to good business relations and successful joint ventures. Many potential business projects are rejected or fail because the French and Americans could not cooperate even when doing so was acknowledged to be in everyone's best interests. We write this book in order to make multicultural interactions with French business individuals both less psychologically frustrating and more mutually profitable.

TWO FRENCH CORPORATIONS

A sense of both the uniqueness and variability of French corporate cultures is found in the comparison of the Michelin Group and L'Oréal Group, both roughly one hundred years old and world-class leaders in their respective industries. Michelin is an example of French technical excellence while L'Oréal exemplifies French concerns for fashion and style. Michelin is also recognized for its tourist guides ("*Le guide vert,*" or green guide) and its gastronomic guides that rate haute cuisine restaurants ("*Le guide rouge*" or red guide). Michelin has been a major arbiter of French tourism and *haute cuisine* since 1900, as well as its premier tire manufacturer. The Michelin tire man (Monsieur Bibendum) is one of the world's most famous brand logos. The name "bibendum" was originally part of the motto *Nunc est bibendum*, Latin for "Now is the time to drink," a curious motto for a tire manufacturer from an US American perspective. (In spite of this very French motto, French law is hard on those who drink and drive.)

The Michelin Group

The Michelin Group, founded in the nineteenth century, is ranked 156 in the largest companies in the world, with revenues of US$13,883 million and over 127,000 employees. Michelin is famous for its secrecy that is notable even among usually secretive French corporations. Michelin's Class B stock is closely held by banks and the Michelin family and thereby avoids the necessity of making the financial affairs of the company public. The general public holds the more-traded Class A stock, but still is not privy to much internal information. A former company president, François Michelin, once went six years before giving an interview to a news reporter. The first non-family member to become a managing partner did so only in 1986. In 1987, Michelin executives invited security analysts to a hotel in Clermont-Ferrand for a financial briefing and a champagne lunch; but the analysts were not invited to tour the factory and offices because no outsiders are allowed on any company grounds except the test track.

Edouard Michelin, the current head of Michelin and great-grandson of one of the two brother founders, sees his role as continuing this tradition of secrecy, making Michelin the "most Japanese of all French companies," and also more efficient in the US American fashion.

Edouard Michelin has introduced a modified form of Taylorism wherever feasible to make labor more productive. This mix of French, Japanese, and US American techniques has made Michelin the world's foremost producer of tires in spite of very stiff competition from Japanese and others.

Edouard's father, François Michelin, remains in a management post at age seventy-three. The company is completely family-owned and there are no outside major shareholders, while most subsidiaries are wholly owned by the company. The holder of the most senior executive post, Edouard Michelin, is addressed as *"patron."* The term is an affectionate slang equivalent to "boss" or "chief." Power, as is typical of many French family-controlled corporations, is highly centralized in the *patron*, who combines the responsibilities of chairman, CEO, and president.

Michelin's managers are paternalistic in the traditional French manner and the company personnel form a corporate family. While the government has taken up many of the social welfare functions once offered by the company, Michelin still operates a hospital, a sports complex, and company stores. Clermont-Ferrand, home to the company's headquarters, still has the characteristics of a Michelin-dominated company town. Employment is for life in the Japanese tradition, and there is a great reluctance to lay off workers, although the company dismissed 15% of its workforce in 1991 in the face of a major recession in the tire market. To reinforce this familism, most workers in the past were recruited from the Auvergne region, where the company was centrally located before becoming a global concern. The administrators avoid Paris and see Parisians as superficial and decadent. The company is uniquely very provincial in its outlook.

Workers at all levels are given great autonomy and latitude in how they do their job. In the words of Jean-Louis Barsoux and Peter Lawrence (1990: 155), workers "are allowed to inflate their jobs to their natural limits. A job definition is determined by the particular aptitudes of its incumbent." This policy is more typical of US American corporations than of French ones. Unique among French companies, Michelin allows its administrators to encourage workers' suggestions and bottom-up communication.

In the German manner, Michelin stresses the manufacturing and production divisions and remains high in R&D expenditures, with an employment of over 4,000 scientists and researchers. The company is very French in its unwillingness to expand too fast and executives avoid diversifying. Michelin remains focused on its core interest of tires. When Michelin's research engineers develop non-tire technology, it sells that knowledge rather than exploit it in-house.

L'Oréal

The L'Oréal Group, founded in 1907, is ranked 186 among global corporations, with 1999 revenues of US$12,784 million and 49,150 employees. Just as Michelin is a world leader in tires, L'Oréal is a world leader in cosmetics and personal care. The French government has declared L'Oréal a national treasure and therefore it cannot be bought by a foreign concern.

L'Oréal employees are expected to dress fashionably, and managers pay close attention to the style of office decorations. Even machines and work areas have an aesthetic as well as a functional dimension. There is as much concern placed on appearance as on practicality.

As with Michelin, L'Oréal executives stress research and development and company philosophy encourages trend setting. Unlike most French companies, L'Oréal also stresses marketing as much as research, with one of the largest promotional budgets among French companies. Managers consciously pride themselves on their "American" emphasis on marketing, an aspect of commerce that French corporate leaders tend to ignore. François Dalle was president and CEO of L'Oréal during the 1960s and 1970s. Dalle earned degrees in law and philosophy but did not attend one of the elite *grandes écoles*. In an interview, Dalle made the then unusual, for a French corporate leader, statement that (Pirouret, 1968:103; translation by the authors):

Our key [to success] rests in these two words: research and *market-ing* [emphasis in the original]. But the two terms influence and interact with each other.

There is a familial character to L'Oréal that is similar to that found at Michelin. There are policies of lifetime employment and extensive internal promotion that are rare in French corporations. Even burnt out employees are kept on, as this very Japanese-type quote by a L'Oréal executive indicates (Barsoux and Lawrence, 1990: 172):

> I am attached to those who have spent their working lives with the company, because I can identify with it. Being grateful to those who have helped build the company is simply a matter of fairness. But it is also in our interests to stand by them; if we sacrifice the older managers, the younger ones will have no faith in the company.

L'Oréal is also unique in that most senior executives are not graduates from a small number of the elite *grandes écoles*. Recruiters seek out a wide variety of prospective employees irrespective of the prestige of their educational institutions. Employees are encouraged to rely on their intuition more than their logic, another characteristic seldom found in French corporations. Often, facts are relegated to secondary importance after personal feelings in making decisions. Executives are also encouraged to take risks.

An exception to this reputation for flexibility is L'Oréal's experience in Asia. At first, company representatives refused to adjust for local tastes and sales were low. At the same time, L'Oréal executives were willing to adopt mass-market techniques when they entered the US American market. They also understood that US American consumers were more brand loyal than Europeans, and promotional campaigns stressed the recognition and loyalty of L'Oréal brand names among potential consumers. L'Oréal's advertising strategy is also unique in France in its emphasis on the development of an international identity. Advertising often has non-French models to stress L'Oréal's global image. L'Oréal has adopted the slogan "think globally and act locally" with a vengeance seldom seen in other French corporations.

In general, organizational structures differ in France and in the United States. US corporations tend to be less centralized and workers are expected to follow corporate rules. French corporations are more centralized and leaders have more personal autonomy to change procedures and goals. US Americans are more goal-oriented while French workers emphasize prestige and respect (Trompenaars, 1993: 267-8).

As the above examples of two similar yet different French companies show, the analysis of multicultural work-related behavior patterns is not yet scientific. For purposes of this book, we base our descriptions of French work culture on information that is as reliable as we can find. However, we also rely on personal reports and anecdotes from those who have dealt with French businesspersons and who have lived in France. Experience is always the best teacher in global business, and learning from others' mishaps lessens the possibility of making the embarrassing mistakes implicit in all multicultural situations. The French call these anecdotes and personal accounts *petites histoires* and use them frequently. They are very useful when they are guided by general principles. We will present the results of surveys of workers' attitudes as well as more theoretical concepts whenever appropriate. The emphasis of this book, however, is how the French behave when they conduct business and how they expect others to behave.

We do not recommend that those conducting business with French colleagues try to become totally French in outlook and behavior. Not only is this almost impossible, but it can become counterproductive. But understanding how and why French businesspersons behave makes for better business and social dealings. All national groups have strengths as well as weaknesses. The challenge is to learn how a national group behaves and then selectively adopt what is useful.

Euro Disney

An example of this cultural selectivity is found in the experiences of Euro Disney (formerly Disneyland Paris). The theme park is located twenty miles from Paris and opened in 1992. This Disney theme park is an example of the dangers of cultural ignorance as well as the advantages of cultural adaptation. An article in the prestigious French newspaper *Le Monde* in 1998 described Euro Disney as "a continuous example of arrogance seldom seen in France." Among the "cultural arrogance" examples given were:

- Excessively high entrance fees (225 francs or roughly forty-five dollars)

- No picnicking allowed

- Dress codes for personnel, including no long hair for men

- American administrators

US Disney officials also found European visitors liked long lunches, with wine and beer; Disney had assumed that, like US Americans, Europeans would prefer quick, non-alcoholic meals, especially while on vacation. Nor do older French people like to eat food with their hands, and the commonly hand-held foods popular in the United States did not sit well with Europeans. Disney was therefore forced to add eating spaces to its restaurants and expand its menus. More seating was also added to accommodate more-than-expected seated diners who stayed at their tables longer since Europeans customarily take one to three hours to eat meals. On the other hand, Europeans are used to using open spaces for their picnics for which they bring their own food supplies. Disney's policy of forbidding guests to picnic on lawns and other green sites angered many Europeans. Potential visitors were also deterred by what they perceived as high entry prices. The ticket price for adults of roughly US$45 was unheard of in Europe at that time and eventually was reduced. These initial policies reduced the number of guests, which has remained below expectations. In order to make the Disney park more acceptable to the French, its name was changed to "Disneyland Paris" (and eventually "Euro Disney") and more activities with French themes were added.

There were other issues. The French like more sedate colors and pastels than Disney was used to. The primary-color patterns successful in the United States had to be considerably toned down. French staff did not like Disney's dress code, such as the ban on men's mustaches and long hair, and too-revealing dress for female staffers, which almost resulted in a strike before the park opened. The dress code was quickly abandoned for the most part, though observers note that a "Disney look" can be found among most of the salaried personnel. Disney obviously won that battle by being more diplomatic and less confrontational.

In the United States, family-oriented facilities do not generally offer alcoholic beverages; in Europe, children are allowed to enter bars and often drink small amounts of alcohol (sometimes watered down) at family gatherings. Disney officials also discovered that Europeans are used to walking longer distances than US Americans and they used the internal transport system less than expected. Disney could have conserved resources here. On the other hand, European tourists buy fewer souvenirs, so that source of revenue was smaller than predicted. Disney spent more and received less.

Unlike the Japanese, who prefer a total US American experience in the Disney park near Tokyo, the French wanted more of their own culture at Euro Disney. Euro Disney added themes based on Jules Verne and other French traditions to satisfy French pride in their own entertainment traditions. On the other hand, French visitors liked the Disney themes, though not to the exclusion of their own traditions; they unexpectedly demanded more US-style breakfasts as part of the Disney experience. French visitors were also impressed by the US-style clean and friendly atmosphere they found at Euro Disney. Those who had visited the Disney parks in the United States were disappointed because it was impossible to maintain the same standards of cleanliness in France as in the United States or at the Disney park in Japan. The French population accepts a lower standard of hygiene than do US Americans.

Disney encourages staff and executives to take their families to Disney parks, and the company provides free passes and events for members of the "Disney family." A US American executive located in France was surprised because a close French colleague had not brought his family to the park though the park had been opened for almost two years. The French executive, like others, did not want to mix business and family by attending Disney events with his spouse and children. Disney needed to learn how French workers viewed their work in relation to their families and free time (Schneider and Barsoux, 2003: 28).

Euro Disney attracted almost 12 million persons during 1998, of which one-third were French. The park began earning a profit after two years of losses, which shows that it is possible to adjust to the tastes of European consumers. Euro Disney gained by transferring managerial control from US Americans to French personnel who presumably were more familiar with French leisure behavior. The park is now one of the most popular tourist attractions in Europe, and Disney Studios is considering another theme park near Paris based on movie themes.

The complexities that can be found when studying corporate cultures across national borders are illustrated by André Laurent's (1983: 86) study of groups of managers from different countries. He asked managers to agree or disagree with the following statement: "It is important for a manager to have at hand precise answers to most of the questions that his subordinates may raise about their work." Those who agree with this statement are less likely to disagree with a superior or criticize a leader's decision on the assumption that he would know best. They are also more likely to follow instructions to the letter on the assumption the superior knows more than subordinates. Those who disagree with the above statement would be more likely to question orders, solve problems on their own, and expect more autonomy at work. They would give respect to superiors based more on personal skills than on position; they would also expect to be given more respect for their own skills. Below are the percentages of European and US American respondents who agreed with this statement:

Sweden	10%	Switzerland	38
Holland	17	Belgium	44
United States of America	**18**	West Germany	46
Denmark	23	**France**	**53**
United Kingdom	27	Italy	66

While over half of French respondents agreed, less than one in five did so in the United States. National tendencies to agree or not with the above statement exist, though French managers, so often different, were almost equally split. But they differ significantly on average from all other European groups of managers, as well as the US American managers.

We also believe that language is one of the best tools to foster understanding of a culture and its society. While it is best to learn a culture at the same time as learning its language, a survey of a culture's vocabulary offers a good illustration of its general values. We present examples of French words and phrases that offer insights that help understand French mindsets. We call these examples *les mots justes* (the right words) and they are found throughout this book.

We use the term "US Americans" in this book to denote people from the United States of America because, while it is awkward, no other term is quite correct. The term "American" more properly applies to all persons in the American continent. The term "North American" equally applies to Canadians, US Americans, and Mexicans. In order to be precise, then, we prefer to use the term "US Americans" in order to specify that the culture and nationality we are referring to is that of the mainstream of the United States of America.

1
FRENCH SOCIETY

Patrimony

A central concept of French national character is **patrimony**, or inheritance. The term implies more for French than for English speakers. The French for patrimony is *patrimoine,* which refers to both cultural inheritance on the national level and personal family inheritance in a sense much more inclusive than just monetary considerations. France's *patrimoine* includes all cultural artifacts such as castles, philosophical knowledge, music, living artists, and art in general. These are cultural treasures to be maintained and transmitted to the next generation. Every French individual is expected to become familiar with France's cultural inheritance, which is included in all levels of France's education.

France's intellectual and humanistic traditions, such as philosophy, art and literature are considered central aspects of the French *patrimoine*. Those who are not familiar with French philosophers and artists, as well as famous historical and architectural landmarks, are seen as uneducated and not quite a proper French person. Adults wishing to be respected must be familiar with French culture in all of its aspects. French executives see US American businesspersons as uneducated and ignorant because they know so little of the history of both France and the United States.

Foreigners are expected to be familiar with French cultural heritage. Foreigners who know little about France's past or take little interest in historical sites and French art are in turn given little respect. They are considered both ignorant as well as dull, uninteresting persons. Someone, whether French or non-French, who wants to be respected must be familiar with (or at least pretend to show interest in) the French cultural heritage. French literature contains many examples of characters ridiculed because they were not "cultured" and who expected to receive respect only because of their wealth or occupational successes.

The government considers itself a guardian of the French cultural heritage. Forty percent of all songs played on radio stations must be in French. A certain other percentage of this music must be by French musicians who have not yet had a hit. This law encourages undiscovered talent by offering them a guaranteed audience until, or if, they become recognized by the listening public.

We recommend that those wishing to do business in France read Pierre Nora's (1998) *Les lieux de mémoire* (translated as *Realms of Memory*), a collection of essays in four volumes about important places and concepts in French history. The collection illustrates what is considered significant in French culture. The phrase "*lieu de mémoire*" remains a familiar topic of general French conversation. The work offers insights on French culture and the French are impressed when foreigners are familiar with works on France or by French authors.

According to journalist Mary Burns, the actress Simone Signoret even saw her own memories as a sort of "patrimony," a kind of public property. "My memories don't belong to me," Signoret reportedly said. "The moment one is talking about oneself one is talking about others as well (Blume, 1999: 78).

✦   ✦   ✦   ✦   ✦

The French define France's cultural inheritance as including contemporary artists and living intellectuals. Educated adults are expected to be familiar with contemporary intellectual and artistic movements as well as those from the past. A major insult in France is to be described as *inculte* (uncultured). An indicator of this intellectual concern was the now-legendary television program *Apostrophes*, which ended in 1990. The host, Bernard Pivot, who remains a household name, invited public intellectuals and authors to discuss currently published books before a live audience on Fridays. The show regularly got about 15% of the television audience, which may seem like a low number but was considered good for a talk show about books.

Film is taken very seriously in France and called the "seventh art." French viewers consider movies to be more than merely entertainment and the government subsidizes filmmaking as it does other art forms. Knowledge of current and classic films is useful for conversation during and after meals. French film focuses on describing family issues, social relationships, and the human condition, usually from tragic and ironic perspectives; car chases and extensive violence are seen as frivolous and for viewers with immature tastes. The French consider most US American films as either for immature audiences or naïve because most film endings are positive (more like fairy tales than real life). The French like films that stimulate and challenge established ideas, usually through extensive use of dialog. French films offer excellent clues to the French national character; foreigners who find French films "weird" or "boring" are missing the point.

The exploitation of film as entertainment is linked to Hollywood, and the most popular films shown in France are made in America, but the French like to remember that cinema was originally a French invention and is now an art form, and a good conversationalist must be able to discuss films seriously.

Business leaders are influenced by the concept of *patrimoine* in several ways. French CEOs and executives often see their companies as entities they have "inherited" and should pass on intact to future generations. This attitude makes them risk-averse and conservative. They are less likely to take chances and prefer slow growth to innovation. They respect traditional ways of doing business and hesitate to adopt new strategies. This respect for tradition encourages looking backward rather than forward.

French also react negatively to threats to France's economic *patrimoine* and this makes them among the most chauvinistic of Europeans (chauvinism, another French invention, is named for Nicholas Chauvin, who was intensely but naively patriotic). The French view competition from foreign countries as a cultural as well as an economic threat. The French consumer-affairs Minister regularly criticizes US American companies for their attempts to "Americanize" French consumer habits.

An example of this view is the French intellectuals' hostility toward US-style quick food establishments in France and the general support for José Bové, a French farmer who has become a national hero thanks to his attack on a local McDonald's. Bové is not a stereotypical farmer living in a backward part of rural France. His parents were researchers at the University of California at Berkeley for many years; the son also lived in California as a boy. The resistance to standardized US American products, especially food, is found in all levels of French society.

Even though there are over 750 McDonald's outlets in France, McDonald's is seen as representing the Americanization of French tastes and therefore non-French in character. McDonald's symbolizes industrialized agriculture in which quality no longer counts, values associated by the French with the United States of America. Jean-Pierre Poulin, a French sociologist, notes that when French people are spotted eating at McDonald's, they act as though they have been caught exiting a theatre showing pornographic movies.

A recent example of the seriousness of French *patrimoine* is a ruling by the French court that French DNA samples are part of French culture and cannot be exported, in the same way that valuable works of art cannot be sold abroad. An American company wanted to purchase a privately owned French institute in order to collaborate on genetic research and to map out human genes. The French company had already collected blood samples from members of over one hundred French families. This valuable supply of genetic material would be analyzed using the most modern US-made technology. The issue became a scandal during the late 1990s, when French politicians denounced this potential "loss" of French DNA material, and the merger never took place (Rabinow, 1999).

Many French managers have been educated in university programs emphasizing the idea that protecting France's *patrimoine* is more important than corporate profits. Most of these business leaders view themselves as administrators/technocrats whose purpose is to promote national welfare. They are suspicious of free enterprise as selfish and a threat to French cultural traditions. Corporations, they feel, exist to serve national rather than personal goals. While younger French corporate leaders are more profit-oriented than older leaders, many still remain loyal to more traditional values, and they hesitate to appear to be less nationalistic than their superiors.

In a study of "new" managers, a French sociologist found that they felt that more traditional managers and executives ridicule their profit orientation. They also felt that they had to explain their attraction to corporate profits within a national framework (Grosset, 1970: 100). While this study is dated, many if not most, of today's French managers still hesitate to appear to be solely profit-oriented.

◆   ◆   ◆   ◆   ◆

Henry James, an American author who spent much time in France, published <u>The American</u> in 1879. The novel concerns an archetypal self-made businessman who goes to France to find a trophy wife. He is surprised that the woman he proposes to, from an old, established family, rejects his offer even though he points out that he can buy her everything she wants or needs. The story focuses on the cultural misunderstandings of an American businessman who gradually comes to comprehend the French value system. The novel is still relevant today and offers a cautionary tale for all who would operate in French society.

✦   ✦   ✦   ✦   ✦

Education, Hierarchy, and Rules

The French evaluate people largely in terms of social class membership and education. Contemporary French society is highly stratified, and France remains the most stratified country in Europe. This stratification of French society is based more on social, cultural, and educational factors than on wealth, and lifestyle is more important than income. Gopnick (2000: 124) writes that "most Americans draw their identities from the things they buy, while the French draw theirs from the jobs they do." A 1997 international survey compared wage gaps between department heads and lower employees, excluding executive salaries, in five countries. Below are the wage differences between each country's best and worst paid workers:

Germany	2.25	**France**	**3.45**
Japan	2.75	**USA**	**4.71**
Great Britain	3.35		

The figures above indicate the highest-paid German department head earned only 2.25 times as much as the lowest-paid employees, while the difference among US Americans was the highest (4.71 times as much). France was fourth largest in disparity. By the same token, French chief executives receive a mid-range pay package compared to chief executives throughout the industrial world. However, income taxes and standard of living costs are higher in France than in the countries with the top five pay packages, so French chief executives would rank lower in terms of absolute take-home pay. Absolute money is not as important, however, as lifestyle and education.

✦   ✦   ✦   ✦   ✦

AVERAGE TOTAL PAY OF CHIEF EXECUTIVES OF
INDUSTRIAL COMPANIES, 1998
INCLUDES BASIC PAY, BONUSES,
PERKS, AND STOCK OPTIONS

USA	**$1,072,400**	Canada	$498,118
Brazil	$701,219	Mexico	$456,902
Hong Kong	$680,616	Japan	$420,855
Great Britain	$645,540	Germany	$398,430
France	**$520,389**	S. Korea	$150,711

<u>Source</u>: Bryant, 1999.

French corporations resemble France's social class structure in the social origins and class-dictated behavior of their members. Top-level officials in government and business are almost always from the upper class; personnel in each lower administrative level reflect France's social class hierarchy.

A very successful individual can raise his original place in the social hierarchy by a few minor sub-levels, but will generally not be able to raise his social class membership from one major social class to another.

Foreigners who do not behave in ways appropriate to the upper classes from which the executive class is predominantly drawn run the danger of not being taken seriously by French decision-makers.

The social status of an individual is largely based on level of education (and type of schools attended), knowledge of French culture, and lifestyle. These class markers develop early in life and derive primarily from one's family and its resources. In theory, all students can attend the schools that train France's elite if they can pass their entrance examinations. The French view their system of education as an example of a meritocracy. As a result, the French take education very seriously. Harriet Welty Rochefort (1999: 27) notes that when she would drop off her children at primary school in France, she would tell them "Have fun," but the French parents around her were telling their children to "Be good." The French word for "good," *sage*, has connotations of being polite and obedient, as well as wise.

The expenses of attending the proper schools are beyond most French parents, however, and most students do not have the ability to pass the entrance examinations successfully without proper coaching (which is expensive). School is too demanding to allow students to meet their educational costs through part-time employment. Students wishing to attend the schools that train the elite must be well familiar with two foreign languages, for example. This almost always necessitates spending several summers in foreign countries to become immersed in their languages. This cost is often too high for most French parents. The best programs that prepare students for the entrance examinations of the elite schools are all private and their tuition is very high. A major expense of raising children involves their education.

There are three results of this emphasis on social class background. First, the French are less impressed by achievement than are US Americans. A person's status is almost fixed at birth and later firmly established according to the prestige of schools attended.

The French distinguish between universities and the so-called *grandes écoles*. Anyone with a baccalaureate degree, which requires passing a tough examination that many fail, can attend a university. While the baccalaureate exam is taken at the end of high school, it is equivalent to having achieved two years of study at an average state university in the United States. French universities themselves are over-crowded and impersonal. They have high dropout rates because up to eighty percent of high school graduates pass the baccalaureate examination and are therefore entitled to attend a university.

Napoléon I established the *grandes écoles* during the early 1800s to train France's leaders, primarily the government, scientific, and military elites. The system evolved to include all leaders, including those in private industry. Graduates consider themselves the nation's elite in a society that respects higher education. For the last two hundred years, cadres have been given the task of managing and modernizing the French economy, and they have up to now been successful in doing so.

For most French people, a degree from even the most prestigious French university is not the equivalent of a degree from one of the *grandes écoles*. The importance of being accepted into a *grande école* is illustrated by the fact that tuition is free and students even receive a salary. By contrast, the non-elite French universities charge higher tuition than their US American public university counterparts.

❖   ❖   ❖   ❖   ❖

The future existentialist philosophers Jean-Paul Sartre and Simone de Beauvoir both took the highly competitive advanced *aggrégation* teaching degree in 1929. The jury agreed that Sartre and Beauvoir were the top two students that year but had to decide who would place first and second. Beauvoir was the youngest in her class and the jury members agreed that she was the better philosopher. But they decided to give the top honors to Sartre because he had been a student at the École Normale Supérieure (one of the *grandes écoles*) and Beauvoir had not. He was deemed superior on the basis of his school (and gender) rather than his performance (Bair, 1990). Such a decision today would cause a national debate but would probably be the same. Graduates from *grandes écoles* are often defined as superior regardless of their performance later in life.

◆   ◆   ◆   ◆   ◆

Jonathan Fenby (1998: 72) summarized the premium placed on intellectualism in France in his description of the mindset of the graduates from the *École Nationale d'Administration. L'ENA*, as this most prestigious school is commonly called, graduates one hundred students a year, and all are destined to become the top of France's elite:

> The aim of ENA is to teach its students how to order and present their ideas, how to produce a seamless presentation on any subject under the sun in which style vies with substance. From any set of data, the true graduate of ENA, or Enarque, should be able to extract a convincing case for either side in an argument.

The most important moment in a person's life is graduating from the *grande école*. Almost no other future success can equal having become a student accepted in a *grande école*. France's leaders form an elitist group with shared educational experiences. There are roughly 184 *grandes écoles* with an average of 400 students each. The rulers of France form a small network of "old boys" trained primarily in mathematics and who excel in test taking and argumentation.

The failure rates in *grandes écoles* are very low because students are rigorously tested before they enter a program. This practice is the opposite of that in the United States where students are continuously tested after acceptance through course examinations. At graduation, all students in the *grandes écoles* are ranked in order of their class standings. Those ranked highest generally get their choice of the best available jobs. Even those who rank lowest find comfortable lives awaiting them.

Consequently, acceptance by a *grande école*, after passing very competitive examinations, establishes the candidate's social status for life. French managers reward educational background and seniority more than individual achievement, though this practice is slowly changing. Having graduated from an elite school ensures a successful career irrespective of personal effectiveness. Graduates are immediately given preferential treatment, including certain promotion.

Graduates from elite schools have been rigorously selected, and they form the most intelligent and well-educated group in France. In turn, the fact that they are considered superior tends to encourage hard work on their part to maintain that reputation. Today, these graduates are increasingly being judged on their accomplishments; they are also being increasingly evaluated in terms of the profit they develop when they work in the private sector. However, there is still a residue of the traditional respect for this elite because of their education rather than their accomplishments.

The respect given to this elite is such that those French who believe there is a crisis in France look to them to develop strategies to enhance French economic and cultural glory. Others blame this elite for whatever occurs in France. The two-hundred-year-old tradition of defining this educational elite as France's leaders, for good or bad, remains strong.

The most prestigious educational institutions in France include the École Nationale d'Administration (ENA), which trains the political elite nicknamed the *énarques*; the École Normale Supérieure, which trains teachers and intellectuals (*normaliens*); the École Polytechnique, which trains engineers and mathematicians (the *polytechniciens*); the Corps des Mines, which admits only the top students from the Polytechnique; and the Institut d'Etudes Politiques, which functions as a preparatory academy for the ENA. The selectivity of these *grandes écoles* is illustrated by the fact that only 120 students enroll each year into ENA; there are probably no more than 5,000 ENA graduates living today, and most if not all are or were in positions of authority.

The first consequence of this hierarchy, based on class and education, is that corporate workers find it easier to talk and deal with their peers than with superiors and subordinates; French corporate communication channels operate better horizontally than vertically. There is little informal interaction between persons from different administrative levels since each level has its own lifestyle and interests reflecting French society's social class hierarchy. Consequently, vertical communication in a French company is formal and rule-bound. The US American custom of dealing with subordinates in an informal manner is counterproductive among the French and they resist this type of behavior. The French see informality across bureaucratic levels as potentially insulting unless the participants are close friends and the situation is informal. However, few executives and managers would have friends in the lower levels. Foreigners doing business with French individuals are also expected to maintain a certain amount of formality during business hours.

The second consequence of the French emphasis on social inequality is that the French tend to evaluate others in terms of character and social class background. This type of social judging results in the French evaluating others largely through first impressions of language, dress, and other visible social cues that define social background. Even today, French firms seldom reward workers on the basis of their individual productivity; pay is based on rank and position rather than work-related performance (d'Iribarne, 1989: 25).

The film *The Taste of Others* (*Le goût des autres*, director: Agnès Jaoui) focuses on the head of a company who has not risen to the top through the usual channels. At first, the film presents him as something of a boor: he fumes at the prospect of having to sit through a play by one of France's most respected tragedians, Racine; his language is not cultivated enough and he uses too many gestures. Yet his tastes begin to change when he unexpectedly becomes infatuated with the lead actress in the play. He tries to develop an interest in modern painting, learns English, and even writes poetry. He finally explains to his manager that the reason he always seems to be putting him down is that he is intimidated by this employee who has had all the advantages of a *grande école* education. The film offers a sympathetic and often subtle analysis of the social connotations of taste in contemporary France.

US Americans tend to evaluate others in terms of their achievements. They mention their achievements as soon as they can to make good impressions. By contrast, the French are less impressed by achievement other than education and think that a person who mentions past achievements is bragging. This attitude is one reason why French CEOs never publish their incomes to the general public and annual reports never disclose executive pay packages. There is no motivation to publicize executive compensation since pay among French executives is based on seniority and education rather than performance.

First impressions, then, are very important; those planning to deal with French businesspersons should look their best, speak as well as possible, and remember that first meetings give the French the basis for their evaluation of others.

The major complaint of foreigners doing business in France is that the French can easily find a reason for not doing something. The French are the opposite of the Japanese in this respect: Japanese find it difficult to say "no": by contrast, French often find it easier to say "no" than "yes." This is due in large part to the many rules and regulations that French functionaries theoretically have to follow. There is also a reluctance to be too active since any action has the possibility of failure. By the same token, few managers are encouraged to show initiative. Inaction is safer.

- "Any problem, however complex, can be solved by failing to take a decision"
- "Beyond the fine art of getting others to do things, is…allowing things to do themselves"
- "Better to do nothing than disappoint"

<u>Source</u>: Barsoux and Lawrence, 1990.

The French emphasis on hierarchy and obedience to rules leads to what Alain Peyrefitte describes as the "culture of irresponsibility": office holders often find a rule to defend inaction and avoid doing something they don't want to do. It is easy to say "no" and avoid taking responsibility.

There are three major reasons for this inaction. The first is the claim that a proposal is "unclassifiable" or "outside the rules." Since bureaucrats interpret the rules that dictate their behavior, it is easy for them to resist change by saying that a petition or proposal is not covered by the rules. An idea that is truly innovative by its very nature is not covered in the rules and will have difficulty being accepted.

Second, there is less chance of being blamed for inaction than for action. As in bureaucracies throughout the world, French bureaucrats avoid action unless it is dictated by the rules. A civil servant's career advances more by avoiding blame than by being innovative.

Third, position holders wish to maintain a sense of individualism by ignoring requests for action. Bureaucrats do not see themselves as having to obey their superiors. They see instead their responsibility as the administration of rules and regulations. French workers of all types and organizational levels ignore orders they feel are outside their boundaries of responsibility. Below are findings from European social surveys by a German public opinion survey firm measuring French insistence on individualism and autonomy (Barsoux and Lawrence, 1990: 7):

Proportions of employees who accept the statement: "Basically, I will carry out instruction from my superiors":

Denmark	57%	Spain	29
England	49	W. Germany	28
Ireland	45	**France**	**25**
Holland	39	Italy	24

Note that French and Italians are least likely to feel that their responsibilities involve primarily an acceptance of their superiors' authority. The same survey asked the reverse of the question above as a check on the response validity of the attitudes being measured:

Proportion of employees who accept the statement: "I only follow the instructions of superiors when my reason is convinced":

France	**57%**	England	34
W. Germany	51	Holland	33
Spain	41	Ireland	26
Italy	39	Denmark	21

The French and Danish samples of employees are the most consistent. The Danes are most likely to follow superiors' instructions and the French least likely to follow instructions. French office holders need to be convinced to perform a task.

The tables above indicate an independence among French workers that they guard jealously. D'Iribarne (1989) found that French managers did exhibit initiative when they felt it necessary. In one case, d'Iribarne observed a manager authorize an order because the person in charge was not available to place his signature. The manager knew what should be done to facilitate work and felt confident enough to place his signature even though this was not within his responsibility. This sense of independence among French workers can result in high efficiency. French workers use their initiative when they wish. This is one reason why it is necessary to establish personal relations with one's French counterpart; they can facilitate work if they accept and respect you.

Cooperation

A distinctive contrast between French and Anglo cultures is that members of the latter have a much greater cooperation ethic. French workers are not expected to cooperate with others on a voluntary basis; instead, they are expected to seek their individual interests. Just as the French elite was trained to be highly competitive during their educational formation, managers see others as potential rivals more than partners.

This tendency to view others suspiciously is much more prevalent among French than among US Americans. Ronald Inglehart has surveyed the extent of volunteerism in a number of countries. Inglehart's World Values Survey found that French adults were among the least likely to join voluntary associations. By contrast, US Americans were most likely to become members and to work for the common good. There is a strong volunteer, cooperative tradition in the United States that is absent in France. Below are the proportions of adults in the two countries who are members of and perform unpaid work for volunteer associations (Lenski, 1996: 2789):

	Proportions of adults in selected voluntary associations		Proportions of adults doing unpaid work	
	U.S.A	France	U.S.A.	France
None	18	61	40	65
Professional Orgs.	15	5	5	3
Social Welfare	9	7	6	5
Religious Orgs.	49	6	29	5
Sports or Recreation	20	19	8	6
Political Parties	14	3	5	2

Note that French are much less likely to join professional organizations than US Americans: their sense of individualism extends to all aspects of their lives in addition to work. Americans form a nation of joiners more willing to work for the common good while the French avoid volunteerism. Many French expect the state to provide the initiative for reform and change and they also tend to avoid joining groups that are not based on family relationships. The French feel that any work performed outside the family should be paid or rewarded in some way and that it is not the responsibility of individuals to work on a volunteer basis.

One (small) exception, as the table shows, concerns participation in sports-related organizations. Many French have a passion for soccer (called "*le football*") and cycling, and local and national French team sports have a large following. However, except for professional athletes, the French are more likely to participate in individual activities such as hiking, skiing, and tennis than in team sports. Even world-class French athletes tend to excel more in individual sports than in team sports. Like the Italian teams, professional French soccer teams are known more for the dash and *élan* of individual players than for their team efforts.

This spirit of cooperation among US Americans is also found in work situations: US Americans find it much easier to cooperate than do the French. The French are too cynical and distrustful of others to cooperate or identify with others easily. This cynicism is found in how citizens evaluate their country. During the mid-1990s, samples of adults were asked whether or not they were proud of their country (Lenski, 1996: 51). Seventy-five percent of US Americans said they were; a smaller 35 percent of French adults answered positively.

Cooperation among French managers does not mean sharing problems to achieve a common goal. The concept of cooperation to the French means to *share* a problem in the sense of dividing it up. Cooperation in this context means that a problem's parts are allocated to various parties. Each party is expected to reach a partial solution that is combined by a superior to achieve a common goal. While Swedish managers, for example, work willingly together toward a common goal, French managers are more likely to debate among themselves to determine who should be the leader and therefore best able to allocate duties to the others.

We must add, however, that US Americans are much more litigious than the French. The US has about 312 lawyers per 100,000 population. The corresponding figure for France is 49. This difference in the relative number of lawyers is influenced by the fact that the French distrust all aspects of government, including the courts.

There are three general characteristics of this individualistic aspect of French culture. First, coordination in French corporations is imposed from above. Workers must be told to cooperate. This creates more regulations than would otherwise exist. There is also a need for closer supervision to make certain that rivals continue to work together.

Second, French cooperate when there is a sense of crisis and not before. Managers are expected to seek private goals unless the corporation is threatened; it then becomes disloyal not to cooperate to fight off an external threat. French corporations are scenes of great conflict and division until a crisis exists. The French are motivated to cooperate more by a sense of existing crisis than by a sense that a future danger might develop.

Third, daily cooperation occurs on a voluntary basis when workers understand that cooperation is personally to their advantage. This need for cooperation for mutual advantages results in corporate fiefdoms. These fiefdoms create divisions within French corporations that limit the spread of communication from one group to another. This, of course, necessitates more formal channels of communication and more bureaucracy, otherwise the level of secrecy would be much higher.

The solution for combating these corporate internal divisions and blocked communications is to develop personal relations with influential persons who themselves are members of the most important cliques. This necessitates large amounts of socializing and the exchange of personal favors. Doing business in France with any success demands that outsiders develop extensive networks and become insiders themseves. They must also be able to offer favors in exchange for cooperation.

On the other hand, French managers do not like to be forced to act. Few decisions are made without consulting others who may resist. French managers become diplomats as they try to convince others that their plans should be accepted. This approach necessitates constant compromises since any disagreement among individualists creates resistance. Thus, French managers are not good team members, but they do develop strong diplomatic instincts.

French Distrust

French managers do not make good team members because a fundamental aspect of French national character is a general distrust of others, which often appears as cynicism toward the motivations of others (Peyrefitte, 1981: 24, 167-8). The French assume others will disappoint them because they cannot be trusted to work for the common good, or to act in altruistic fashion. Such views encourage the belief that only a strong authority—and a strong bureaucracy—can regulate affairs among people. This is another reason why the French do not cooperate: they assume someone will want to take some advantage of the team's members for personal gain. Using the plea that "working together will achieve a goal" is not a successful motivating strategy.

Accepting Courtesies

Tradition and formality encourage attention to protocols and etiquette. Being conservative, the French maintain more formal rules of etiquette that have been discarded in less conservative societies. The French follow well known prescribed etiquette, which lessens any possible uncertainty when dealing with strangers and with those from different social and educational backgrounds. Consequently, French businesspersons prefer following rules of etiquette to interacting with others without clear behavior guides (being informal). It is important to know what these courtesies are and how to express them so that a non-French person can offer and receive these courtesies correctly.

Foreigners from less formal cultures should learn the protocols that guide behavior among the French, especially since the French are intolerant of foreign customs. We also suggest that common courtesies offered by French business colleagues be accepted graciously. Otherwise foreigners give the impression that (1) they are ignorant of how to behave properly and/or (2) they seem to reject a colleague's friendliness.

For example, the older or senior person passes through the door first. A French individual who asks you to go through a doorway first is indicating you are an honored guest. It is a grave mistake (*faux pas*) to insist on informality and say that order of precedence is unimportant. Precedent and acts honoring someone are always appreciated and noted. By the same token, the French are easily insulted if proper etiquette is not followed.

Seating is also dictated by etiquette in France. Visitors to an office are asked to sit in a special arrangement indicating rank. Visitors should never presume to take charge and sit wherever is convenient, nor take the liberty to tell hosts where to sit.

The Cadres At The Workplace

One of the most unique elements of French business practice is the presence of *cadres*. The French term has no direct translation in English (and is not the same as the political use of the word "cadre" in English), but it corresponds most closely to "manager" or "executive." The foreign word that most reflects the nuances of the term "cadre" is "mandarin" and leading cadres are often described as France's mandarins. Cadres manage others, make decisions, and represent an elite group ideally working to support France and its culture. They personify the ideals of service and intellectualism.

The French term also has additional legal and social dimensions. Cadres are seen as a distinct third occupational category between workers and employers, though not quite the same as the English term "manager." A person designated as a cadre receives higher prestige, higher pay, higher retirement benefits, and is considered on the fast track for promotion. In exchange, cadres work an average of 66.5 hours per week. Leading cadres work longer hours partly to differentiate themselves from ordinary bureaucrats who maintain a civil servant mentality of watching the clock. Cadres, by contrast, are taught that they are responsible for projects whose completion time is indeterminate and long-term. Like Japanese non-manual workers, French cadres work late and take work home to show their dedication and their usefulness. Like managers and executives, cadres do not receive overtime pay though they are expected to work longer hours than non-cadres.

All of France's decision-makers are *cadres supérieurs* (top-level cadres) who have graduated from the high prestige *grandes écoles*. The few exceptions are those who have inherited their top positions in family-owned firms. However, parents from wealthy families almost always try to prepare their children to enter the *grandes écoles*. Family background and personal wealth mean relatively little unless a person is also a graduate from an elite school. On the other hand, even a recent *grande école* graduate with a temporary lower-level position demands respect. Foreigners often ignore the importance of these elites and fail to give them adequate respect.

There are two ways to become a cadre. A worker can be promoted to cadre status after a few years of apprenticeship. He or she then becomes an *ingénieur-maison* (company engineer) or *cadre moyen* (mid-level cadre) and the cadre designation is specific to that company and not transferable elsewhere. Changing employers almost always means losing the cadre status. Generally, these *ingénieurs-maison* have graduated from lower prestige educational centers and are considered self-educated (*autodidacte*), meaning they have learned their skills on the job and not by attending a high-prestige university. The French consider any person who has talent but has not graduated from a *grande école* as self-educated. Some of these *cadres moyens* did not graduate from a university but have been promoted in-house because of their technical skills and practical experience.

The most common path to cadre status, though, is through graduation from one of France's *grandes écoles*. Cadres who have graduated from the elite *grandes écoles* are designated by law as *cadres supérieurs* to differentiate them from the other cadre category.

The education of cadres is important because originally, the prestige of cadres was based on their being considered as the non-academic intellectuals of the nation. They were given power because it was assumed that cadres knew more and were smarter than any other worker category. In a society where intellectualism is extremely respected, as in France, those defined as more knowledgeable are given both respect and leadership positions.

Future cadres are taught that they are France's elite, and very few leaders in France are not graduates of the *grandes écoles* unless they have inherited their family-owned businesses. Although more cadres are currently pursuing careers in the private sectors, it is important to stress that all graduates are taught they should concern themselves with national goals; their corporate goals should be secondary to the development of French national interests.

From a business point of view, the four most prestigious commercial *grandes écoles* are the *Écoles Supérieures de Commerce*; the *École des Hautes Etudes Commerciales* (HEC); the *École Supérieure de Commerce de Paris* (ESCP); and the *École Supérieure des Sciences Economiques et Commerciales* (ESSEC). These *grandes écoles* and a few others stressing engineering are the source for almost all of France's leaders. Graduates are expected to repay the state for their education through ten years of employment in government; many companies are willing to pay the state the required fee to free a graduate for instant employment outside government upon graduation.

Friendship

Friendship is the major non-sexual relationship that is freely selected by the French. A French individual must accept and be loyal to relatives, but friends are accepted on a voluntary basis. In French, a person "is" a brother while one "becomes" a friend.

Part of the process of becoming a friend is saying "*tu*" instead of "*vous*." This grammatical change in address is part of a voluntary process that indicates an emotional closeness. Only adults who are equals say "*tu*" to one another outside of family members. While friends use the more personal form of "you" it is best to continue with the "*vous*" form until a French acquaintance suggests "*tu*" is appropriate. Often, the more formal "vous" is used in public and the "*tu*" forms are used in private or outside of work. It is a major etiquette fault to use the "*tu*" form and then revert to "*vous*" as doing so indicates rejection of friendship and equality, or that one has made a mistake in the closeness of the relationship, so it is safer for US Americans not to rush into informality when addressing the French.

French individuals already feel that US American friendships are too easily formed and are therefore shallow and undependable. Becoming a friend among French is a process of developing trust over a period of time. Though some friendships are instant among those of equal age, friendships are usually formed over time through a process of sharing confidences and doing activities together.

Many male US American friendships are specialized in that a person's friends may not know one another well. An American man may regularly go bowling with a few friends and play weekly poker games with others: the two sets of friends may never interact. French friendship circles tend to overlap so that the same people are friends together. Becoming a friend with one person often means becoming friends with others.

> Eric Rohmer is one of France's major film directors and known for his "moral tales." One of his most recent films, Autumn Tale, concerns two women in their mid-40s who are old friends. One woman, Magali, has been widowed for some time and is evidently lonely but is doing nothing about it. Her happily married friend Isabelle decides to find her a boy-friend, places an ad in a newspaper, and impersonates Magali in order to interview the men who respond to the ad. When she is confident that she had found the right man for Magali, Isabelle introduces the two. Magali is immediately smitten by the man Isabelle has chosen, and it never occurs to her to be angry at her friend for what US Americans might perceive as her meddling, or for not having consulted her. Conversely, the film *With a Friend Like Harry* (dir. Moll) presents the nightmare of what can happen when a friend thinks he knows what is best for you.

Friendship among the French is also more of a responsibility than among US Americans. Americans are likely to preface a request for a friend's help with "I hate to bother you, but...." By contrast, French friends are expected to be more aggressive and take charge to help a friend in need even before asked. A French individual may say to a friend "I feel tired today." The friend is expected to take charge, saying, "You need a rest; I'll take you to my family's country house and we'll have a picnic. Don't say no." US Americans would feel that this offer was too controlling and treating the friend as a child.

✦ ✦ ✦ ✦ ✦

| *Ami:* | A close friend; French consider only two or three persons as *amis*. The relationship is close and *amis* see each other or correspond frequently. |
| *Copain:* | The French equivalent of "pal." A person has many *copains*. The French feel that US Americans do not differentiate enough between these two concepts. |

✦ ✦ ✦ ✦ ✦

French friends often argue with one another in public. The French like to debate with one another, and arguing with friends is no exception. Arguing is also an indication that, though friends, each party is allowed his or her opinion independent of the other. US American friends are expected to agree with one another and offer more support in public.

French business colleagues avoid developing friendships at work and maintain a formality that would be unthinkable in most other countries. Since friends are expected to help one another, formality at work avoids potential favoritism among those who might develop more personal ties that could lead to manipulation. The French feel that informality at work has the potential of reducing efficiency.

Time

The ways time is used and defined in different cultures can be divided into **monochronic** and **polychronic** (Hall and Hall, 1990). People in monochronic cultures see time as linear and in short supply and therefore it should not be wasted. Monochronics experience time as going in one direction, toward the future. The past tends to be defined as relatively unimportant. Believing time to be linear, monochronic businesspersons seek to be efficient in their use of time and they find it easy to break up time into shorter units. It is easy as a result for monochronics to prioritize projects and schedule a series of tasks according to their importance. Monochronics believe that being on time is honorable and a question of courtesy to others. This attitude encourages scheduling and agenda-making

German, Swiss, Swedish, and US American cultures are the most monochronic cultures in the world. Such cultures are described as "time starved" in that members feel that there is never enough time to complete all that needs to be done. Persons from those cultures are comfortable with short meetings, with detailed agendas, and with planning. They feel rushed and avoid "wasting" and "losing" time. US Americans say that clocks "run" because they feel that one never has enough time to meet goals (in Mexico, clocks "walk"). Monochronics take schedules very seriously and allow agendas to control their lives ("I don't have time for this").

Monochronics like messages that are clear and concise, as well as those that can be read efficiently and quickly. They become irritated when messages are unclear or too complex; they are likely to encourage the use of executive summaries and abstracts in their reading materials.

By contrast, polychronics view time as an ample resource and open ended. There is no need to rush, or to be on time, since there is ample time to do what needs to be done. The French see time as an ample quantity while life and friends are in short supply. There is always time to be polite and enjoy life with one's friends; tasks can always be completed eventually. French executives will insist on a two-hour lunch rather than eat a sandwich and keep working to meet a deadline.

Polychronics also use time in multiple ways; they are comfortable doing several things at the same time. A meeting in France tends to have a flexible agenda and new ideas or proposals are welcome additions. There will often be several conversations at once dealing with several topics. Meetings also often last beyond their scheduled ends.

A polychronic French custom is the interruption of meetings with telephone calls and subordinates who must get advice or a signature immediately from a superior. French decision-makers are relatively few in an organization and are very busy because they do not delegate well. Subordinates must wait for their superiors to make decisions, and this results in frequent interruptions of meetings to get permission on how to proceed on a matter.

French managers almost encourage interruptions because they often become bored with details and procedures. The emergence of crises whose solutions only they can provide will increase the managers' self-esteem and prestige. Interruptions during a meeting merely indicate the importance of leaders as they show that only they can solve urgent problems.

French consider the future uncertain and largely uncontrollable and do not like to plan far ahead or schedule meetings more than a few weeks ahead of time. They take the view that detailed planning is impossible since there are always unforeseen events that interfere with planning. Meetings are cancelled easily and without much excuse. A major irritation to more monochronic and schedule-oriented nationalities such as US Americans, Germans, and Scandinavians is this French tendency to cancel meetings at the last minute.

Scheduling is also seen as an invasion of one's individuality and freedom of action; French executives prefer to react to events rather than to prepare for them. A person who meets a crisis successfully is more respected than someone who avoids the same crisis. Besides, crises are seen as giving life excitement and as a chance to shine as a problem-solver. Leaders who work well under pressure are respected, while the cautious plodder is ridiculed.

Meetings seldom start on time; a fifteen-minute delay is traditional, though there are pressures to make meetings more efficient by starting at the official time. Discussions cannot begin until the highest-level attendee arrives. Since power is centralized, group discussions without their leaders are considered useless, though decision makers often come to meetings to show their independence and prestige.

The French view of time is also reflected in how they view deadlines. There are two types of deadlines, *date butoir* and *date cible*. *Date butoir* is the formal deadline that must be met at the time specified (a *butoir* is a bumper, something that blocks movement forward, such as the bumper at the end of a train track). This deadline must be written in a contract to be effective. The more common type of deadline, *date cible*, is a general schedule that is more indefinite rather than clearly stated; it is a target (*cible*) to aim for, rather than a definite obligation. Often, French manufacturers may understand a contractually specific target date as in reality a general date (*date cible*) that is flexible and approximate rather than a definite date (*date butoir*) stated in the contract. Consequently, missing a specific deadline is considered unimportant, something that should be forgiven. French law does not take much interest in missed deadlines and it is almost impossible to sue for damages due to late shipments, for example.

A noteworthy use of time among the French is the way they view deadlines in relation to quality work. Like the Germans, French individuals prefer late deliveries if meeting a schedule results in poor workmanship. The delay of French workers often results from a concern for a high quality performance rather than from negligence or inefficiency. From the French perspective, it is better to be late than deliver a low quality product. US Americans and British are likely to define late delivery as the result of laziness, inattention, or low productivity. However, missing deadlines by the French may, and often is, the result of wishing to deliver a product as good as can be made. The French are more tolerant of being late than they are of shoddy work. In this context, the French believe there is always plenty of time to perform a quality act.

The French are a mix of monochronism and polychronism. They are on time when a situation calls for strict scheduling (the French train service is a model of punctuality). But they are also occasionally likely not to feel that a situation demands meeting a specific deadline. On balance, though, French businesspersons are more polychronic than monochronic, especially in the South.

US Americans see historical events as interesting or as a source of pride, but the past is not seen as a guide to the present. The term "it's history" means an event is irrelevant and cannot be used to make decisions about present events. By contrast, the French attitude is that the past and the present are closely linked and that the former makes the latter understandable.

The term "recent" for the French may include events that took place a hundred years ago or longer; for US Americans, "recent" is usually a reference to no more than a few months. A practical consequence of this attitude is the French preference for framing current events within the past; present events make more sense if they form part of a continuum with the past. Speeches often begin with historical allusions, and contemporary events are discussed as continuities of the past. The French describe the history of France since 1789 as *histoire contemporaine* (modern history). They see present events as embedded in the past rather than as new beginnings. It is second nature for French decision-makers to be concerned with how their decisions fit in a historical context.

French tend to fear the future and remain traditional or past-oriented. The future is uncertain and uncontrollable; it is better to repeat the past than innovate. As a result of this preference for past stability, the French find it difficult to believe in the benefits of growth and development: it is better to support the status quo than to promote change. There is a strong strain of *neophobia*, or fear of the new, among the French, and novelty and change are feared rather than welcomed. An idea or proposal is more likely to be acceptable if it is presented to the French as an extension of the past and not as a novelty. French intellectuals such as Philippe d'Iribarne describe a major French characteristic as a fondness for moderation; this attraction for "moderation" is in large part a conservative attraction for the past.

This anti-future mindset reflects the belief that change represents rebellion and disloyalty to the more respected past. That is why change in France has often been brought about by violence and social explosions rather than through peaceful increments. A condition has to be extremely bad before reform is accepted, often because of threats of violence; many government and business reforms have occurred in France as a result of demonstrations that threaten possible violence if demands are not met. Short labor strikes and street demonstrations that cause traffic jams are common in France because government leaders are seldom inclined to change the status quo unless they see no other alternative.

The solution to this reluctance to change is to convince French decision-makers that a proposal is necessary to avoid chaos and calamity while it furthers French honor and glory. As we have pointed out earlier, French executives enjoy working within crisis conditions and they will enthusiastically become involved in projects that promise to end a crisis; this is when French leaders do their best. On the positive side, a sense of crisis can result in innovative behavior and more intense work patterns.

Government and business schedules use the twenty-four hour system to denote time, where 10:00 means 10 a.m. (and 10 p.m. would be written as 22h.). The French are more likely to use the 12-hour system for social occasions. It is best to check which system the speaker is using, though the correct time can usually be determined by the context of the time mentioned (not many business meetings would be scheduled for 10 p.m.).

There are two French uses of time that are very irritating to those from more monochronic cultures. First, the French believe that there is plenty of time to study a proposal very carefully. In contrast with those from more monochronic cultures, French decision-makers are willing to spend more time on planning and study, and they are willing to delay action to allow for careful study. US Americans, on the other hand, prefer to start acting as soon as possible and to worry about details later. Too much planning is seen as a waste of time; mistakes can always be corrected later. By contrast, French decision-makers prefer taking their time analyzing and studying a proposal and delaying action.

Second, French businesspersons want to establish personal relationships with business associates. There is always a period where very little business is discussed while partners become familiar with one another. US Americans who feel time starved and in a hurry to begin and end business discussions feel very frustrated when decisions that would take a few days to complete in the United States or Canada never really begin until the socializing stage is completed. Europeans in general, and French in particular, distrust strangers too much to conduct business with those they don't know.

Vacations and Holidays

There are other holidays besides those that are designated officially (see below), including Midsummer's day also known as St. John's and the "Fête de la Musique," when musicians perform in public areas late into the long summer day. Many communities still celebrate their traditional holidays, such as a local Saint's anniversary. The city of Orléans, for example, sponsors a holiday for the anniversary of the day Joan of Arc liberated the city with a parade and fireworks. Mardi Gras (Shrove Tuesday) is often celebrated by visiting and receiving friends.

OFFICIAL HOLIDAYS

New Year's Day	Jan.1	Bastille Day	July 14
Easter Monday		The Assumption	Aug. 1
Labor Day	May 1	All Saints' Day	Nov. 1
Victory Day	May 8	Armistice Day	Nov. 11
Ascension Day	5 weeks after Easter	Christmas Day	Dec. 25
Whit Monday	8 weeks after Easter		

Family celebrations remain important in France. A number of holidays are associated with special foods or other traditions (like Easter eggs in the US). The lily of the valley flower ("*muguet*") is associated with Labor Day (May 1). The "*fête des rois*" (literally "the feast of the Kings," but better known in English as Epiphany) is celebrated on January 6 with a special cake. A (dried) bean is baked into the cake and whoever receives the slice with the bean is crowned king with a paper crown.

Baptisms, *communion solonnelle* (confirmation) for twelve-year olds, weddings and funerals for family members are seldom missed and are valid reasons for absenteeism from work. These almost always occur during the weekend, but they may demand absenteeism on Fridays to travel to a ceremony's location. Birthdays, on the other hand, are seldom celebrated in France. Traditionally, people celebrate and receive gifts on the feast day of the saint for whom they were named. All first names in France are traditionally saints' names (for more on names in France, see Bernstein (1990) and Blume, 1999: 156-60).

◆   ◆   ◆   ◆   ◆

LES MOTS JUSTES

- *FAIRE LE PONT* (make a bridge): Workers take an extra day off when a holiday falls on a Thursday or Tuesday to make the weekend longer. These "bridges" are often listed in work contracts. Managers and executives often take their "bridges" as a privilege of their rank.

- *MOIS DE CONGÉ* (the month of holiday): the major annual holiday lasting four to six weeks, suggesting that any shorter period cannot be an adequate holiday.

◆   ◆   ◆   ◆   ◆

The most common holiday periods are July and August. Most workers receive four to six weeks (some even more) of annual paid holiday and three of these weeks must be, by law, taken together. Many stores and businesses close entirely during the month of August, and many factories are on reduced schedules during the summer months.

Workers who do not take their longest vacations during August take off during June or July. The summer months, as a result, find a large part of the labor force absent for some time. It is best to avoid making deadlines and appointments during June through August. Workers also take shorter holidays around Christmas and New Year and during Easter. Contemporary French are becoming accustomed to taking shorter vacations, however, the month-long summer vacation is still enjoyed by most French adults and children.

PAID VACATION DAYS
PER YEAR, 1994

Bombay	39	Milan	25
Madrid	32	London	22
Frankfurt	31	**New York**	**11**
Paris	**28**	**Los Angeles**	**9**

Source: Union Bank of Switzerland.
Reported By *Time* September 5, 1994: 16.

There are other holidays and times of the year when absenteeism from work, for women employees especially, is tolerated. The days before the beginning of the school year, called *la rentrée*, involve much preparation, especially for parents of young children. Parents count down from about two weeks before the first day of school; J-10 ("D-Day minus 10") means ten days until the opening of school, and parents begin their preparations for their children's first day of school at that time if not earlier. The highways are clogged with returning children and their parents; stores are often full of shoppers for school supplies. Many workers are preoccupied with *la rentrée* even when they do not take a day or so away from work.

Other special events can cause either absenteeism or inattention to work. Beaujolais nouveau wine is officially available during the third Thursday of November; the tour de France takes place during the end of July and is seen on television or in person by most of the French; soccer championships, local, national, and international, also engross all Frenchmen, especially during the soccer World Cup championships. Parents of high school students are preoccupied during the month of June, when students take the baccalaureate examinations that determine the occupational fate of their children. In some regions, the opening of hunting season or other local festivals may also affect the attendance of the workforce.

Making Appointments

The French do not like to schedule appointments far ahead in the future. They feel that scheduling inhibits their freedom and individuality. They also believe that the future is too uncertain to control by scheduling. It is best to make appointments with the French a few weeks ahead of time expecting the schedule to be changed at the last minute. Since the French work best under crisis situations, they are comfortable with last-minute scheduling changes on the assumption that a crisis has occurred that must be given priority.

Lunch is often a two-hour affair, and workers enjoy discussing the next meal during the late morning, even if such a discussion interferes with business. Appointments are best made for mid-morning and after 2:30. Shorter noonday meals are becoming more common, but higher-level managers still take their lunches seriously. Business may be discussed at the end of a meal over coffee, but lunches are occasions to enjoy food and conversation rather than to conduct business.

Evening business dinners are rare in France. One can invite business associates for dinner, but little business will be discussed; the occasion is social rather than business oriented. Business breakfasts, still considered an American custom, are becoming more accepted although they are disliked by older French managers. They take place in the larger hotels that have breakfast facilities; food is usually served buffet-style.

Measurements

France, like most countries in the world, is on the metric measuring system. It is best to present all measures in the metric system when dealing with Europeans, including the French. Not using the metric system in publications may cause delays while all measurements are translated into their metric equivalents. Conversion charts are widely available, and the metric system is easy to learn, since it is based on the decimal system (units of ten). Also, temperatures in France are routinely expressed in centigrade not Fahrenheit (freezing occurs at 0 degree in centigrade, rather than around 32-33 degrees, Fahrenheit), so if you are checking the weather report in order to decide what sort of clothes you might need for a business trip, be sure to note which system is being used.

TEMPERATURE CONVERSION

Centigrade=(F-32) x .555
Fahrenheit=(C x 1.8)+32

Attitudes Toward Work

A French newspaper once contained the question "Are the French Lazy?" The answer was typically French: No, but they're a little sleepy. The answer is an overstatement, although it is true that work in itself has little meaning and seldom motivates the average worker. A French person works for prestige, for power, or for meeting an interesting challenge, or from a sense of duty.

The typical French worker prefers a job that is secure, even if such a job offers less income. Even-well educated persons may hold jobs for which they are over-qualified in exchange for absolute job security. This attitude of preferring security over high pay is an indication of the widespread fear of change, or neophobia, held by the French, as discussed earlier. The popularity of government employment or of positions in companies partly or completely controlled by the French government, despite the relatively low pay they offer, reflects the government policy of lifetime employment.

Companies that have a policy of lifetime employment pay less and promote almost totally on the basis of seniority, though they also offer complete job and career security. Even privately held companies in France are restricted in their ability to lay off or dismiss workers. The result is that most French workers enjoy lifetime job security.

French culture denigrates work unless it offers prestige. This attitude reflects an aristocratic tradition that a person should avoid working if at all possible: the French work to live rather than live to work. Essentially, those who have to work have less prestige than those who work only because they want to do so. The ideal economic situation for most French would be the possibility of living on return of capital and *rentes* (revenues) rather than earning their incomes by holding jobs. Following a more aristocratic tradition that remains in force today, inherited income is given more prestige than earned income.

At the same time, the French are also aware of their strong tradition of anti-monarchist and anti-aristocratic feelings manifested in the democratic belief that, in the final analysis, money alone is not what is important. These sets of attitudes are examples of French contradictory beliefs that confuse foreigners.

French managers work long hours and frequently take work home. However, the French in general do not respect those persons whose main interest is only work; workaholics are ridiculed rather than respected in France. People should work hard when necessary, but they also should enjoy life, and a large part of enjoying life is intellectual activity. Colleagues like to discuss with one another food, sports, politics, and the arts as well as task-oriented topics.

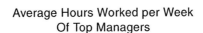

Average Hours Worked per Week
Of Top Managers

Britain	45.1 hours/week
France	**44.3**
Spain	42.6
Holland	36.9

Source: Woodruff, 1999.

Work should be interesting and challenging. Dull, manual, and repetitive duties are considered appropriate only for those who have no other choices, mostly because of a lack of the proper level of education; those who have choices in work tasks avoid technical, detailed activities ("*fastidieux*," the French cognate word for "fastidious," means "boring" in French). Executives respect those who work with style (*élan*) rather than efficiency.

The French attitude toward work is also shown by the government's current attempts to shorten the workweek to create more jobs and reduce France's unemployment rate of roughly 11%. The legal system has mandated that the workweek for all workers except top senior executives be decreased from its current 39 hours to 35 hours. By contrast, higher-level workers, especially all types of cadres, work long hours and are workaholics by any country's standards.

The French government will soon begin to sue all workers, including specialists and managers, who work for pay more than the legal 35 hours weekly or more than ten hours in one day. During 1999, Bernard Rocquemont was fined US$16,000 for allowing his 1,700 salaried employees to work a total of 8,000 hours beyond the legal limit (Woodruff, 1999). An executive of Thomson-CSF was also fined US$7,800 because his employees had worked overtime. More serious violations can be punished with jail time of as much as two years.

Managers are expected to install time clocks so that workers who work more than 35 hours can be identified and sent home to reduce their working averages. Workers who work more than their allotted average of 35 hours are expected to use their "credit" by staying home until their average weekly workloads are normal, or following the French customs, by taking longer lunch hours or vacations. Companies are offering workers longer vacations while keeping the workweek as long as before. Some workers will now receive 25 extra vacation days annually (in addition to the usual five or six weeks due all workers) in exchange for a 35+hour workweek.

The shortened workweek and its related record keeping have made French managers aware of the need for more efficient uses of time. Meetings are now more likely to start on time rather than fifteen minutes late, and agendas are more likely to be better developed and followed to a greater extent than they were in the past.

Another attitude toward work that influences business-related behavior is the French attitude toward selling and salespersons. Salespersons are not highly respected in France. Based on an aristocratic tradition dating from when those few persons who could afford to buy many goods were part of the nobility, sales persons are still seen as lower class merchants who don't contribute much to society. Charles de Gaulle once undiplomatically dismissed the Japanese ambassador to France as "a transistor salesman."

The French, like Germans, respect those who make things or are managers more than those who sell or are in marketing. Contemporary French tend to treat sales persons with formality and social distance; they also expect the seller to be more polite than the buyer. Customers do not expect a clerk to be personal by using first names or making jokes. Customers and sellers both use more formal terms of address and avoid personalizing the relationship.

LES MOTS JUSTES

- *Se décarcasser*: to work one's butt off. Literally: to "decarcass" oneself
- *Se démancher*: to work hard. Literally: to disjoint oneself
- *Gratter*: to do a lot of paper work. Literally: to scratch

French negotiators often try to frame negotiations so that the other side is the petitioner trying to initiate business relations, thereby giving them lower prestige and influence. It is easier to say 'no' or to make additional demands if your counterpart is seen as the one who is asking for an action on your part. You will be given less respect if you seem to be the salesperson or petitioner. It is better instead to gain the upper hand by acting as if you are granting a request rather than offering a product or service.

A consequence of this, besides a more formal relationship between seller and buyer, is that those who are considered to be sales personnel are given little respect by senior managers (cadres) and their ideas and suggestions are seldom taken very seriously.

The salesperson/buyer relationship tends to be long-term and personal. These ties can only be developed slowly over a long period of time and by developing mutual respect. A salesperson who is brash, pushy, and not intellectually interesting will be avoided, while a soft sell approach, lots of entertaining and interesting conversations, lead to contracts. The salesperson who is hurried, assumes equal status with customers, and as a result makes a negative first impression seldom succeeds in France.

On the other hand, French businesspersons pay special attention to salespersons with whom they have developed personal (though formal) relationships, and will favor these with advantageous contracts and respect. Salespersons who leave their companies generally take their customers with them since a buyer's loyalty is to the salesperson rather than to the employer or company.

Attitudes Toward Money

The French stereotype of a US American is in part a person who talks and thinks about money and about little else. Americans are also seen as living to work in order to earn more money rather than taking the time to enjoy life. The French categorically reject this materialism and find it vulgar and unsophisticated.

For their part, French individuals seldom refer to the cost of objects. They may know the monetary value of objects, but they consider it bad taste to describe an object by its value or cost. A French hostess would never mention how much her eighteenth-century dining table cost; her guests should know the table's value and age without being told.

Money is important to US Americans because wealth signifies success, though often money has to be spent in visible ways to give the person prestige; the miser who does not display his wealth (i.e., worth) through conspicuous consumption is seen as antisocial. The American saying "If you're so smart, why aren't you rich" indicates the significance of wealth.

By contrast, the French see an interest in money as uncouth behavior. French executives would not be as interested as US Americans in a project that promises "only" a large profit. Proposals should offer prestige to those involved and stability for the company as well as a profit. Projects also should be framed as helping France and its society. The US American customs of closing plants that no longer provide a profit or dismissing underused workers are not only illegal in France, but considered antisocial. French executives would hesitate to add workers who might become redundant after a project is completed.

US Americans should try to avoid mentioning money and profit when talking with French individuals. French executives are concerned that a proposed project achieve profits, but decision leaders will be reluctant to mention financial issues until very late in the negotiations.

SUGGESTED READINGS

Aselin, Giles and Ruth Mastron (2001) *Au Contraire: Figuring Out the French.* Yarmouth, Maine: Intercultural Press.

Axtell, Roger E. (1991) *Gestures: The Do's and Taboos of Body Language Around the World.* New York: John Wiley & Sons.

Barthes, Roland (1972) *Mythologies.* New York: Hill and Wang.

Bernstein, Richard (1990) *Fragile Glory: A Portrait of France and the French.* New York: Knopf.

Fenby, Jonathan (1998) *France on the Brink.* New York: Arcade Publishing.

Moll, Dominic [director] (2000) *With a Friend Like Harry (Harry un ami qui vous veut du bien).*

Peyrefitte, Alain (1981) *The Trouble with France.* New York: Knopf.

Platt, Polly (1996) *French or Foe? Getting the Most out of Visiting, Living and Working in France.* Skokie, Illinois: Culture Crossings.

Zeldin, Theodore (1996) *The French.* New York: Kandasha American.

2

LANGUAGE AND COMMUNICATION

The Importance of Language

The French consider their language a central part of their cultural heritage, their "*patrimoine*," and fluency in French is a major part of how French and non-French are evaluated. It is almost impossible to be fully accepted, or respected, when one does not speak French well.

The French government considers itself a guardian of the French language. Thus it is illegal to use foreign words or mixtures of languages, such as *Franglais* (a mixture of French and English), in public advertising or other official discourses. Disney Corporation was sued in a French court because its Paris store contained several dozen articles out of several thousand with labels in English rather than in French as required by law. The University of Georgia was also sued because a French website about its summer program in France was not available in French.

The importance of language facility among the French is such that they admire and like persons who can argue skillfully and with style. Someone who disagrees and expresses different ideas is seen as interesting. Those who always agree are evaluated as uninteresting or hypocritical. This attitude causes conflict when the French deal with US Americans. US Americans want to be liked, and they tend to agree with persons, or at least they seek common ground, often through compromise. By contrast, the French do not seek to be liked; they would rather be admired and respected, especially for their knowledge and lifestyle, and agreement does not impress the French.

French and US Americans also differ in how they express themselves. US Americans define intelligence in terms of a person having a large amount of facts that can be used for specific purposes. Intelligence is seen in large part in being able to recognize relevant facts and being able to use this knowledge. Intelligence testing generally takes the form of measuring how many isolated facts can be recalled and whether the test taker can use this knowledge in an appropriate and practical manner. US Americans are empirical-inductive in their thought: they gather as many facts as they think would be useful. The act of thinking to US Americans is largely the collecting of relevant facts and avoiding theoretical speculation. US Americans tend to be leery of ideas divorced from facts. The common US saying cited in the previous chapter, "If you're so smart, how come you're not rich" reflects this attitude that knowledge should lead to concrete results, in this case wealth.

The French by contrast are Cartesian in their thinking style, which is to say skeptical and deductive. They believe that knowledge is developed by questioning established truths rather than solely by collecting relevant facts. An intelligent person to the French is someone who is critical and can point out weaknesses in others' thinking rather than knowing mere facts. A person is defined as intelligent when he or she can express these ideas brilliantly and in an entertaining manner. This respect for general principles over facts may be one reason why so many ideas were developed in France while other countries found practical uses for these ideas. France is one of the few countries where milk is not pasteurized, for example.

Salvador de Madariaga, in his study of national character, summarizes that the British are people of action, the Spaniards people of passion, and French people of thought. As an example of this stress on thought over facts, the term *c'est impensable* (it's unthinkable) means that something is "not possible" or that the speaker doesn't want to waste time considering the proposal. The French are also deductive in that they begin an argument by stating general principles; they then fit facts into their theory. Sociologist Philippe d'Iribarne (1989) describes the French style of thinking as focusing on "great principles and small facts" while ignoring the practical.

French education emphasizes intellectual development in which students are taught to manipulate ideas to increase their aptitude for reasoning; this is one reason why logic and mathematics form the central core of elite educational programs. Below are sample questions of the baccalaureate taken by high school students. These questions and others are provided by the Ministry of Education on a website to help students prepare for the examination. Note the abstract and philosophical nature of the items.

✦ ✦ ✦ ✦ ✦

TEST QUESTIONS FOR PART ONE OF THE BACCALAUREATE
(Taken when students are seventeen years old)

- Explain why, according to Tocqueville, democracy is always threatened wherever it develops?

- Define "liberty." Theme: Liberty consists of following one's reason, which should be developed.

- The ephemeral is that which does not last. But the concept of duration poses problems: what does not last is transient, by which we mean one lives only a few instants, but the concept of the "instant" is also difficult to conceptualize....The problem concerns the meaning of "value." What values illuminate the above concepts?

- Do increases in the population of a nation encourage or handicap economic development?

✦   ✦   ✦   ✦   ✦

Using the French Language

Viewing the French language as a national treasure, the French appreciate foreigners' attempts to speak French, but become irritated by those who speak French badly. Foreigners will not be treated completely as equals worthy of respect unless they speak the French language fluently.

French is not an especially difficult language for English speakers to learn, though it does take considerable time and effort to speak French well and to be easily understood by a French audience. Many non-French persons speak French well, and roughly twelve percent of adults in the European Union feel able to carry on a conversation in French. Most French businesspersons speak English with some facility, and thirty percent of the French general population can converse in English.

Younger French are more fluent in English. Often, however, senior executives will pretend not to speak English well if in fact they do. When they socialize they almost always revert to French as more comfortable and expressive. It is much better to be able to speak French fluently and not have to depend on a translator.

All French respect an *animateur*. This word is difficult to translate directly into English but it means someone who can bring things to life, make them animate and interesting through language. An *animateur* is a person who makes difficult topics understandable. The topics may be either technical or philosophical. The French respect ideas and they respect those who can explain philosophical abstractions and technical treatises. This is a reflection of the respect given to those who are highly educated, including specialists. A person who can explain his specialty to a general audience is respected in France. This superior knowledge gives status and encourages thorough study of a subject matter. A reflection of this respect for *animateurs* is the saying *ce qui n'est pas clair n'est pas français* (what is not clear is not French).

Businesspersons cannot rise to the top unless they are *animateurs*. A foreigner who is both fluent in French and able to discuss abstract ideas well is given respect and listened to. Those who can give brilliant presentations are much less likely to be ignored than those who are inarticulate.

✦ ✦ ✦ ✦ ✦

A sign in the German-speaking area of Switzerland contained the same message three times:

German version: Walking on the grass is forbidden

English version: Please do not walk on the grass

French version: Those who respect their environment will avoid walking on the grass

<u>Source</u>: Victor, 1992: 156-7.

✦ ✦ ✦ ✦ ✦

The French tend to be rude only in public, as when a clerk does not offer proper service. By contrast, French are polite in private since offering proper hospitality is vital for one's reputation and self-esteem. Private areas include meetings, letters, and telephone conversations; consequently, business conversations tend to be formal and polite. It is considered inexcusable and impolite (considered almost the same thing) to be critical or too informal in face-to-face conversations and meetings. Correspondence needs to be formal rather than informal; all hints of criticisms should be muted.

US Americans, because of their higher levels of individualism, tend to use the pronoun "I" more than do French conversationalists. The French language is famous for the use of impersonal expressions such as *"on"* (one), which, in casual conversation at least, has virtually replaced the first person pronoun "je" (I). The French prefer to de-emphasize individual achievements since these are less important as a basis for social prestige. They do not seek to make themselves look good since style is more important than achievement (Levieux and Levieux, 1999).

The French are less likely to offer personal information or ask personal questions because they respect ideas and how they are expressed more than achievements. The offering of personal information, or the discussing of one's achievements, is seen by the French as boasting rather than as trying to achieve personal contact. While a US American is likely to say "I like the summer best," a French individual would say "Summer is the time for vacations" and let the others assume that he likes summers because of vacations. Note how the quote by the French speaker also generalizes and more impersonally establishes a general principle while the US American quote is more personalized.

In addition to avoiding personal remarks, speakers should also avoid discussing money directly. Reflecting an aristocratic heritage, the French view discussing money as too materialistic and *bourgeois* (middle class). A cultured person should not be overtly concerned with money and seldom discusses financial affairs. Wealth is best inferred by dress, house, and general life style, though not necessarily by conspicuous consumption.

Cynicism

The French agree with foreigners who find French national character very cynical. French cynicism is a deep-seated distrust of others' motives and human nature in general. They assume that people are devious and cannot be fully trusted. The French are tolerant of others, but they are also suspicious of others. French cynicism encourages a distrust of optimism and statements of friendship. It is counter-productive to state, for example, "You can trust me" because the French do not trust the motives of strangers. Nor do they accept at face value statements that are too optimistic. Optimism, the French feel, indicates either a naïve view of the current situation or an attempt to hide the truth. Either way, there are grounds for suspicion.

Thus, it is better to be as factual as possible and avoid statements that the French would not believe. Such statements include not only statements of friendship, but also any statement that is optimistic, such as, "I think we made lots of progress today" or "Our negotiations should be completed soon." Such statements will be ignored by French individuals as insincere or unbelievable and will not influence their behavior.

French businesspersons also tend to ignore verbal invitations such as "let's do lunch sometime" because they assume that they are merely verbal noises made for the sake of politeness. By contrast, the respect for the written word encourages the French to accept written statements. A written statement that the writer wishes to have a meal with the correspondent will be taken more seriously than a similar statement presented verbally. On the other hand, it is necessary to follow through on any invitations in order to be taken seriously in the future.

The French do not trust accounts that are too positive and certain. They feel that an account of a business proposal described as a "sure thing" or "the greatest deal of the century" denotes hypocrisy or naivety. The French distrust sugarcoated descriptions; they are too pessimistic and cynical to be so certain of a positive outcome. It is best to mention any possible difficulties with a proposal. They will feel insulted if their careful analysis of a proposal contains weaknesses not mentioned earlier.

In addition, the French dislike others' boasting about their accomplishments. They feel that bragging probably hides weaknesses and uncertainty and that the speaker boasts because of ignorance or lack of proper etiquette. Boasting is also seen as an indication of immaturity.

The French are not much interested in others' past accomplishments in business and French businesspersons do not take seriously the argument that a project will be successful merely because the presenter had been successful in the past.

Legislation of Language

The centralization of power in French history and culture, along with the role of government in preserving the national "*patrimoine*," can be illustrated through attempts to legislate the usage and development of the French language itself. Language is seen as a concern and responsibility of the authorities. Ever since the founding of the prestigious *Académie Française* by King Louis XIII's minister Richelieu in 1635, the French have struggled with the question of whether and to what extent they should be prescribing and policing so-called proper speech and vocabulary (Landick, 2000).

In recent years, there has been no shortage of government intervention into questions of linguistic practice. Most of these interventions are responses to the perceived threats to the language caused by *Franglais*, the hybrid of French and English that results from borrowings, importations, and neologisms derived from English and grafted onto the French language.

An example of borrowing technical terms into French is the fast-evolving domain of computer terminology. The French language quickly developed its own words for many of the basics of computing: "*un ordinateur*" for "computer," as well as "*le logiciel*" for "software" and "*l'informatique*" for "computer science." However, it is common to hear references to "*le computer*" and "*le software*" due to the dominance of English in the computer field.

In another example of English influence, French words may be used but the English concept is retained and translated into French, as in the case of "*une souris*" (the French word for "mouse," both the rodent and the computer kind). In yet more blatant examples of word borrowing, the English word is adopted wholesale into French, with a French pronunciation of the English word. The worldwide "web" becomes "*ouebbe*" although there exists a perfectly good French word that could be used ("*réseau*" or "network"), and "*surfer*" becomes the activity one carries out on the "*ouebbe.*"

Moreover, the borrowing of words, particularly English ones, is further encouraged by the social perception of higher prestige the use of English confers upon the speaker. An illustration of this borrowing can be seen in the United States of America where the use of French words in a conversation can make the speaker appear more sophisticated (as in Jim Henson's Miss Piggy of the Muppets using "*moi*" instead of "me"). The French also will imitate the speech of American movie and television stars to show their cosmopolitanism. Thus, the French borrow (or invent, as in the case of "*le footing*" for jogging) American-English words to gain prestige. Whether because of American domination of entertainment and popular culture or British snobbery and aristocratic values, English offers a certain *cachet* (as Americans might say) to many segments of French society.

In response to these linguistic problems, French government officials have intervened out of a desire primarily to protect their linguistic "*patrimoine*" (cultural inheritance). This concern has led French government officials to pass a series of laws aimed at regulating linguistic practices, such as the *loi Toubon* of 1994. This law extended the *loi Bas-Lauriol* of 1975 that had banned *Franglais* (along with all other foreign words or even syntax) from all texts such as advertisements, packaging, warranties, contracts, and any public document, including outside advertisements such as billboards (see Landick, 2000 for further details). This action is understood as a form of consumer protection and fraud prevention. US Americans advertising their products in France must be especially careful to avoid English and *Franglais* in their advertising. Government officials search for such illegal actions and the importer is likely to be heavily fined, or worse. The law has not been without legal challenges, but this has not stopped cases from being prosecuted.

The issues of *Franglais* and the use of foreign words raise two important issues for those doing business in France. First, the national debate about language illustrates further the importance in French culture of patrimony in the widest sense. Language is viewed as a natural resource and, unlike in the USA, where natural resources are sold off as private property (so that McDonald's "owns" the phrase "happy meal"), language for the French is a natural resource that belongs to the country as a whole and merits protection. Foreigners who do not show respect for the French language will not be successful in France.

Second, *Franglais* may be both an asset and liability to an Anglophone doing business in France. It is an asset because in specialized areas dominated by Anglophones, one's French counterparts are likely to know English technical terms, thereby facilitating communication. *Franglais* can be a liability because it cannot be used in official (or even any public) business-related activities. All contracts, advertising, websites, etc. must be conducted in French.

Conversation

As noted earlier, the French take very seriously the art of conversation. To be taken seriously, one must be able to discuss certain topics with flair. French businesspersons feel that their US counterparts are boring and unintelligent because they only wish to discuss business topics.

Certainly knowing about recent sporting events is a start. But while a thorough knowledge of the history of America's World Series in baseball may be sufficient to bond with a business associate in the United States, it will take more in France. The French have little interest in US style football, baseball, or basketball. One should, however, know something about European sports. The Olympics is always a good topic of conversation if the foreigner does not brag too much about his country's successes and the relative lack of medals won by French athletes. Other socially correct sports themes are world soccer, especially since the French "Cinderella" team won the world cup in 1999. Knowledge of the *tour de France* bicycle race is a must when visiting

France during July. However, the fact that an American won the tour in 1999, 2000, 2001, and 2002 makes the topic a sensitive one and should be glossed over. Rugby and tennis are good conversational substitutes.

A US American expatriate in France should also make a point of glancing at some newspapers before meeting French colleagues and of following the news as often as possible. The *International Tribune*, an English-language newspaper available throughout Europe, is a good starting point, as is the CNN international news channel often available in French hotels. You will pick up more of the necessary knowledge of French current affairs from a French language newspaper, however, and reading local material offers the opportunity of learning the vocabulary needed to discuss current affairs correctly. Politics is always a favored topic among the French, and they enjoy criticizing government policy and activities. An important aspect of citizenship is being informed on political affairs, and the French consider someone who is uninformed on politics as an irresponsible citizen as well as dull.

Expect to be able to discuss everything from the latest election to the essay subjects given in the baccalaureate exams given nationally to all high school seniors hoping to go on to college. The Ministry of Education publishes former examination questions as well as ideal answers to guide future test takers, and the topic is covered extensively in the press at the time of the baccalaureate exams in June.

The first step in being a good conversation partner is being well informed. One must also be able to offer opinions. A good opinion is not one where there is agreement among discussants, but is based more on the skill with which one defends it. In France, style wins over content almost every time. Playing devil's advocate with *flair* (and good humor) will earn you more points than simply siding with the majority.

Many elements go into a good defense, including knowledge. A central part of any debate is the ability to cite precedents and historical examples. A discussion of shoes, for example, should begin with the style of Roman shoes and the role shoes have played in the history of France. The knowledge of what French King Louis XIV and his official mistress wore would gain debate points. Historical precedents, no matter how remote, cannot be underestimated; they are never irrelevant and familiarity with historical details gives you prestige and respect.

Wit is also central to being respected as a good conversationalist. A witty and spirited presentation may gain more prestige than a dull but correct list of facts. Business presentations should be kept to a minimum with as little data as possible. Hand out all the relevant technical data for study later. Since the French distrust figures, data are very carefully analyzed, partly to discover errors, and taken very seriously. The French educational system strongly develops analytical abilities, causing the French to study empirical facts in a very critical manner. Presentations themselves should contain more style than facts; facts become important later.

There is one final warning about the attributes of a good conversationalist. No matter how brilliant and witty, the good conversational partner does not simply hog the limelight and offer a monologue; conversation is interactive. Conversation is an activity everyone plays cooperatively. Someone who shuts others out is not playing fair.

CONVERSATIONAL RULES

- Do not ignore others while you flirt with someone next to you
- Do not pull one person out of the group for a private conversation
- Do not engage one person in a long conversation; don't monopolize
- Keep circulating
- Cede the floor to someone else after making a point

- Know how to change the subject when a topic gets dull or too sensitive

- Engage others in conversation

Conversations about one's personal religious beliefs are taboo, unless one knows one's interlocutor very well (in which case the confessional mode may be appropriate). Many US American Christian denominations have an evangelical aspect, and US Americans feel that, if their religion brings them joy and comfort, it is an act of generosity, and even a duty, to let others know of the solace religion can bring. To the French, religion is a very private matter, and not an appropriate topic for the workplace. US American discussion of religion may be perceived at best as another example of American arrogance ("I know best"), at worst as insensitive. It may help for US Americans to remember that as little as sixty years ago, one's religious affiliation (if one were Jewish, for example) could cost a French person their life. A seemingly innocent question to a US American—"what is your religion?"—has been a matter of life and death numerous times during the history of France.

Conversational sound levels are lower among French than among Latin and US Americans. The exception would be during meals or during informal leisure conversations that take place usually while at home with friends and relatives. Only children and adolescents raise their voices in public, and they are often reprimanded for being too loud by parents and even by nearby strangers. French children are taught to be quiet in public and noisy US American children seem "spoilt" or "immature." French consider US American tourists rude and objectionable because they are louder than is considered appropriate. Ideally, no one should hear private conversations while speaking in public.

Conversations during business meetings are also muted and participants seldom raise their voices. Discussions in offices are also softly spoken. One seldom hears others' conversations while passing groups of workers. Being loud is considered disrespectful and rude. One never raises one's voice to older and more senior persons.

The "Tu" and "Vous" Forms of Address

The French language reinforces the recognition of formal and informal relations with the *tu/vous* phenomenon. *Tu* is the familiar form of "you" and *vous* is the more formal form. More formal societies such as Germany, Italy, Russia, and Spanish-speaking countries still pay attention to this distinction while more informal societies seldom differentiate between a formal and informal second person. The formal "you" in Sweden and the informal ("thee") in the United States have pretty much disappeared from common speech.

The French film *La cage aux folles* depicts and mocks a very traditional French family in which the father is the Minister for Morality. This presentation—although stereotypical—is useful for English speakers who want to get a sense of what an extremely traditional French family might be like. The fact that all members of the family address each other with the formal *"vous"* serves to remind Anglophones of the subtlety and importance of the *tu/vous* distinction.

Saying *tu* to a person indicates a close relationship usually limited to family members and close friends. Office colleagues may use the *vous* form for years and never reach the informality that allows the use of *tu*. The *vous* form is mandatory in French business. The superior decides when a relationship is emotionally close enough to use *tu* instead of *vous*. Foreigners who know little French but want to use a few words should always use the *vous* form. The French realize that many foreigners do not understand the subtleties of the *tu* and *vous* protocols. They are usually willing to ignore grammatical errors, but they do notice these errors, and they find an inappropriate use of *tu* mildly offensive. For one thing, children under the age of ten use *tu* indiscriminately; adults doing the same, even if they are foreigners, run the danger of being seen as being childish and immature.

The *vous* form indicates respect as well formality. The French use the *tu* form when talking to children and animals. To address a person with *tu* might be seen as insulting or inappropriately informal. If in doubt, it is better to say *vous* to everyone since this is less likely to give offense. The slang term "*ta mère*" ("your mother") is insulting in part because of the use of the *tu* form.

LES MOTS JUSTES

INSULTS

- *Ta gueule*: Shut up. Literally: Shut your muzzle
- *Ferme-la*: Shut up. Literally: Shut it

Business correspondence always uses the formal *vous* unless a very close relationship has already been established. Older French executives frequently call no one at work *tu*. By contrast, younger French work colleagues are increasingly using the *tu* forms of address with one another since doing do makes working together more relaxed. As a result of the political upheavals of May, 1968, the use of the *tu* form is taken by some as an ideological insistence on equality among workers in the same way Russian and Chinese Communists called one another "comrade." French companies that have adopted US American or Japanese forms of working are more likely to encourage the use of *tu* among work-equals, though older and higher-level employees resist this informality. Even if you hear other people using *tu* with each other, do not assume it is acceptable for you to do the same. Often, former schoolmates use the more impersonal *vous* at work and *tu* when socializing away from work.

An indication of the importance of the *tu/vous* form of address is found in a language custom in the *grandes écoles*. All students and graduates automatically acquire the right to use the *tu* form with all other students and former students, no matter the differences in prestige, age, or position. Richard Bernstein (1990) recalls a conversation between President Mitterand and Giscard d'Estaing in which both addressed each other with the *tu* form for this reason, despite their extreme political rivalry that would make the *vous* form seem correct. US Americans tend to think that friendliness is a virtue and that sending signals that one is friendly and non-hierarchical cannot possibly cause offense. Some therefore think that the *tu* form is a good opening conversational gambit. Nothing can be further from the truth in France.

Body Language

Body language of French individuals is also more formal than among US Americans. Body posture remains formal most of the time, and the French dislike the US American practice of "getting comfortable" by slouching, lounging, or placing feet on desks or arms of chairs. While a certain amount of informality is tolerated among friends, a general rule for US Americans to follow is to be more formal than relaxed. French adults relax with friends and relatives but very seldom with business colleagues. Relaxation of body posture among business associates indicates a lack of respect for others and a disinterest in the business at hand.

French children are constantly told to "stand up straight" and "sit up straight." Adults are also expected to maintain formal postures at work. The French see casual postures as uncultured and childish behavior.

After introductions, guests wait to be invited to sit down; guests in France do not take any initiative in others' presence. After receiving permission to sit down, do not slump in the chair or move its location. Seating is placed where the host wants it to be located, and moving a chair to better talk to someone is an insult and improper behavior for guests.

Hand gestures are also restrained, especially during business hours. Foreigners hold the stereotype that the French speak with their hands, much like Italians and other Mediterranean people. The French strongly feel that only those from the lower classes use much gesticulation. Northern French and Parisians use more restrained hand gestures than those in the South, but southerners are stereotyped as being less serious and less business-oriented. Too much hand gesturing signifies a lack of education and sophistication, and demeans the individual. Those who need to use their hands to communicate must not be very verbally expressive, it is felt, and the value the French place on articulateness has already been stressed. Traditionally, clowns and fools make outlandish gestures to reinforce their negative images. On the other hand, the authors of this book use more hand and body gestures and facial expressions when they talk in French than in English.

Observe French political and business individuals. They move their hands to emphasize what is being said, but the gestures are seldom expansive, and hands seldom wave around far from the body; a slight shrug of a shoulder or shoulders is considered expressive. The rule is, again, use restraint. The French use their hands more during meals and informal conversations, but even then their hand gestures are more restrained than foreigners' stereotypes.

There are a number of French gestures that express emotions and messages. A shrug while holding the palm up and away from the body means *qu'est-ce que tu veux que j'y fasse?* Or "what do you expect me to do about this?" Two fingers placed against nostrils means "It's so easy I can do it with my fingers up my nose." Rubbing palms together means, "I wash my hands of it." Pointing the forefinger up in the air parallel to one's temple is a call for silence because the person is going to say something very important. The last two gestures can be seen during business discussions and should not be ignored. Other gestures are found in Laurence Wylie and Rick Stafford's book *Beaux Gestes*.

GESTURES TO AVOID

- The gesture with the thumb and forefinger forming a circle means "nothing" or "worthless." It can also mean *au poil!* or perfect. It is sometimes considered vulgar.

- Slapping a closed fist on an open palm is vulgar.

- Snapping the fingers is vulgar and insulting. Be careful when counting on your fingers. The French start counting with the thumb.

Women in France are expected to use more subdued body language than men. Women do not sit with their legs apart. This is allowed for men, though to a lesser degree than in the United States. Women do not move their elbows far from their sides. They are also expected to dress more formally than men and to keep their voices lower when they speak.

Like Europeans in general, the French shake hands often. They exchange handshakes when meeting for the very first time and also when seeing one another for the first time that day, and when they separate. French handshakes are short and gentle (no vigorous pumping) without much squeezing of the other's hand. The handshake should be firm but gentle at the same time (no "limp fish" or simply pressing of fingers). The participants look each other in the eyes and approach each other so that they are within each other's personal space. They then retreat a half step or so to more normal talking distance. The superior or host holds out the hand first. Women also take the initiative when shaking hands. Those sitting down always stand before shaking hands.

Handshakes should take place immediately upon greeting someone; delay or hesitation to shake hands may be understood as an unwillingness to shake hands and is an insult. French do not wave as a substitute for handshakes; a nod as a substitute for a handshake is also seen as an insult or as emotional distance. If you see a friend or colleague on the other side of the street, it is not unusual to cross the street in order to shake hands, especially if you are the subordinate in the relationship, though this does not entail prolonged conversation; the act in this case is an indication of respect. A person indicates special closeness by holding the other's hand with two hands. This double handshake is done among close friends, especially after a long separation. By contrast, more formal superiors who wish to maintain social distance with subordinates often offer two fingers rather than an open hand.

French body language codes take other forms that are unexpected for US Americans. These differences include the topic of restrooms. To many Americans, the availability of free, clean, and easily available restrooms is a sign of civilization. US American tourists make the lack of modern restrooms in France their major complaint (with the exception of not being understood).

American guests see the availability of restrooms as a sign of hospitality, both in homes and in retail businesses. Hosts in the United

States often give guests a tour of their homes partly to show them the location of restrooms. The assumption is that restrooms are available for the convenience of their guests who need not then be embarrassed about asking to use them. Often a restroom is designated as the "guest bathroom." Guests in the United States are expected to slip away to use the bathroom when they feel the need. No other permission is needed and embarrassment is avoided. This is not the case in France. A bathroom is seldom designed with guests in mind.

Restrooms in French homes are not seen as the property of guests; restrooms are part of the private area of homes that is not available to guests. Business associates, on the rare occasions when they are invited to a colleague's house, do not expect to be shown either the kitchen or a restroom. Only family members and very close friends are allowed the intimacy of informal access to the kitchen or bathroom. The French hold a very negative stereotype of US Americans as persons who want to use a home's bathroom as soon as they enter a house.

French children are taught from an early age to exercise strong self-discipline in terms of bodily functions. The inability to control oneself is seen as childish and marks the individual as immature. A foreigner is placed at a disadvantage if he or she is seen by French business acquaintances as being childish because of frequent requests to use restrooms.

Consequently, the French do not expect that business and houseguests will arrive wanting to use "the facilities." It is not uncommon among French to host a dinner party during which none of the guests ever disappears to the restroom during the entire evening, even after a two-hour, six-course meal.

The point here is that American visitors in France who do not wish to draw negative attention to themselves should consider managing bathroom needs. Try not to use the restroom facilities soon after arriving. It's better to use public restrooms, if necessary, just before arriving at someone's home or office, or even at a restaurant, if you want to make a good impression.

Nudity

In general, the French are more relaxed about nudity than US Americans, who are sometimes viewed as extremely puritanical when it comes to matters of the body and sex. French films and television shows are less likely to be censored because they show naked body parts than their US counterparts. The French are far more likely to reject depictions of violence than of nudity, since the latter is considered "natural," a part of nature (and the French value nature). There is far more tolerance of nudity in advertising, for example, in France than in the USA.

The French consider US Americans too prudish in general, and find scandals such as the President Clinton-Monica Lewinsky affair incomprehensible. When former President Mitterand was buried, his wife asked that his long-time mistress and their child be allowed at his funeral. Her view was that this mistress and child meant much to Mitterand and should be allowed to pay their final respects in public during the official funeral.

On the other hand, the French value formality, as has already been stressed, especially in business culture. Nothing less than proper formal dress and behavior is expected. Even leisure activities such as golf and tennis call for the "correct" attire.

Smiles

Smiles communicate unique messages among the French. The French have a stern or unexpressive look in public or during business hours, since smiles are reserved for friends and relatives. Strangers are given more serious glances or none at all. The French only smile when there is a personal reason for smiling; they do not smile just to appear happy or friendly. Strangers do not have the right to know whether someone is happy or not; nor do the French want to appear friendly towards strangers.

French individuals in public areas do not look as stern as Scandinavians, especially Finns, who are famous for looking dour in public;

French public expressions are similar to the English and Germans. People who smile in public for no discernable reason are seen as untrustworthy or foolish. Pickpockets and other petty criminals are more likely to choose someone who smiles indiscriminately as a possible easy victim. Notice photographs of French politicians: they are likely to look stern and remain unsmiling.

Lack of smiles is customary in business settings. A person is not supposed to enjoy working; work is a duty that one fulfills honorably but not with glee. US Americans feel that work should be enjoyed, and that worker satisfaction leads to higher morale and therefore higher productivity. Workers in France do not expect work to be enjoyable. One enjoys oneself at home and during leisure activities. It is therefore appropriate to look serious during work. Those with responsibilities should look a little worried and harassed, but not very much.

Using The Telephone

Older French managers do not like to use the telephone and many view receiving a telephone call as similar to an unannounced visit. Both are unwelcome. Many also see a telephone conversation as less serious than one that is face-to-face or written. Those who request a commitment from French individuals should rely on written communications rather than using the telephone. In addition, decision-makers do not like to make quick decisions or while talking on the telephone. They resist answering questions that require them to decide on the spot.

A successful strategy is to inform by telephone that you wish something done and then follow through with a fax, memo, or mailed letter. You can suggest you wish an appointment on or near a certain date and then send a hard copy request. This allows the recipient to select one or more dates that are mutually acceptable. An appointment will probably not be made without consulting the superior and aides and asking for a commitment on the telephone is counterproductive and may end any friendly relationship already developed. It is seen as a form of discourteous harassment. Again, suggest orally a tentative date or preference and then send a letter asking for a meeting or decision.

Personal telephone calls are quite acceptable, and the telephone is frequently used in France to maintain personal contact. We recommend frequent telephone calls, even if overseas, to maintain whatever personal relationships have developed. While telephone calls do not replace personal visits, telephone calls are seen as more personal than letters, especially fax and e-mail correspondence.

In the past, all calls, even local ones, were billed by their duration and callers became adept in making short conversations. The French telephone system is now one of the most modern in the world and voice transmission is excellent as well as dependable, unlike in the recent past. France is seventh among the world's countries in terms of the number of persons per telephone line (1.8) and almost equal to the United States (1.6).

France lags in terms of home computers (14th in the world) in part because the French national telephone system gives access to the "Minitel" computerized system, which offers over 17,000 services. The terminal is cheap to rent for all telephone owners and its services involve very small fees for each use. A great deal of information and activities (train and movie schedules, games, weather conditions, theater reservations, even dating services) are available using this computer system that runs off the phone line. The "Minitel" system also supports English language chat boards and services. For many people, it makes a personal computer redundant.

Many French, especially the older generation, continue to view telephones with suspicion. Although the French generally prefer longer to shorter conversations, they developed the custom of avoiding extended telephone calls, and telephone conversations tend to be formal and abrupt. The French also prefer face-to-face conversations and businesspersons are reluctant to call back when a message is left.

In homes, the family telephone is often located in a hallway and is arranged for practicality, rather than comfort or privacy. It is not expected that a person will be on the phone long enough to need to sit, for example. Many older French still think of telephones as only for emergencies or at least only for communicating essential information (as telegrams were in the United States), and not for chatting and socializing. If you are at someone's house, do not ask to use the telephone unless there is an emergency. If it is unavoidable and you have to use the telephone, keep it brief and do not expect privacy. Do not be surprised if your host remains in the room with you.

In the office, a person using the telephone when another walks in will point to the office's clock to indicate the talker will soon be finished with the conversation. The visitor commonly sits in a chair and pretends not to be listening to the telephone conversation.

Despite the reluctance to use the telephone, French phone technology is very advanced. There are many public telephones available throughout France. Most public telephones now take only pre-paid telephone cards (*télécartes*) readily available in most public places, for example in neighborhood *bureaux de tabac*. These telephone cards often carry advertising or other images and have become highly collectible in France as trading cards have become in the United States.

Pre-paid telephone cards are available in 50 or 120 *unités* (approximately $10 and $20). A brief, local phone call may require only one or two *unités*. The 120 *unités* cards are cheaper in the long run: they cost only twice as much as the 50 *unités* cards and often benefit from cheaper rates.

If you are concerned about keeping the cost of calls from public telephones down, ask the person called to call you back; public telephones all have their numbers clearly marked. One can even call overseas in this manner. Overseas calls are cheaper when they originate from other countries. For the businessperson, it is possible to call one's office overseas, give your number and wait for the return call to engage in a longer conversation (make certain your office knows the appropriate area codes for France before you leave, however). This is how most French avoid going through telephone cards too quickly. Almost no one calls collect ("*en PCV*") anymore because this system of cards works so well. As a result, many French have forgotten how to call collect.

Mobile telephones have also become extremely popular in France, in part because the French feel mobile telephones are status symbols of modernity. However, it is illegal to use them when driving an automobile. There are a number of situations in which French etiquette dictates that cellular telephones should be turned off. Sometimes this is announced, but sometimes it is a matter of expected courtesy (at films and concerts), especially during business meetings.

One always says "*Allo*" when answering the telephone. The first thing you do when placing a call is to identify yourself or the agency you represent. For more telephone etiquette and expectations, see Raymonde Carroll's book *Cultural Misunderstandings*.

Communication

The French consider knowledge a source of both power and prestige and they do not share information easily, except with close friends and peers. Receiving information is also seen as a loss of control, as the one making a request is admitting he is more helpless than the one who presumably has the information.

French businessmen are famous for not volunteering information until asked. Not only is knowledge power, but the French would hesitate to volunteer information for fear that, first, the other person does not need the information; and second, the other person already has the information and offering the information may seem like an insult. Third, the one with the information may not trust the other and may not know what will be done with the information. Fourth, asking for information threatens the superior's authority and autonomy unless that information is strictly associated with duties being performed. There is a strong sense of *méfiance* (mistrust) in the French national character.

Fifth, information is difficult to obtain, and there is a reluctance to make information transfer too easy: let the other make the effort to get the information! All French decision-makers went through a very rigorous educational system that demanded tremendous efforts to become educated. You must pay your dues, too, and get your information the hard way: earn it.

Getting information from French colleagues demands a need to know and a personal relationship where trust has been established. The French will gladly offer information if these two conditions are met and they are then asked for the information. But they must first want to give information; information sharing is seen more as a friendly gesture than a responsibility.

By contrast, French individuals feel overwhelmed by the information US Americans give them. Americans are willing share any and all information they have while French individuals prefer to give information on a limited need-to-know basis. The French tendency is to keep secrets in contrast to the more open attitude of US Americans. There is the French attitude that public information is not reliable; they place more trust in personal communication with experts and friends.

Americans also like to present written information; French prefer their information in verbal form from persons they know. As a result, French develop personal sources of information by constantly cultivating the friendship of those who have information they might need in the future.

However, a French person who is willing to give information to someone also feels an obligation to be thorough and as helpful as possible. The individual with information now has the responsibility to give information since he has in essence been honored by this request for information. Many US American tourists have been astonished by the positive responses of Parisians who are asked for directions. Unless the Parisian does not want to give any information at all, she is likely to give detailed information and even take the tourist to the street corner to point out the appropriate route. In the same way, friends are expected to take every request for information, or aid, very seriously.

Expatriates in France need to cultivate personal channels of business information or they will be given only the inadequate information available to the general public. It is also better to ask many questions when asking for information on a topic on the assumption that the information will be specific to the question and therefore incomplete. The French do not follow the US American custom of offering large amounts of information to be sorted out, arranged, and even ignored according to the needs of the one requesting the information.

Researchers comparing working patterns throughout the world note that French workers seldom talk informally to those above and below them in rank. By contrast, US American workers assume more equality across work levels. They assume that everyone is approachable, resulting in more informal communication among workers in the United States. Those working with French workers should remember that subordinates seldom communicate directly with superiors on their own initiative, since that violates the top-down bureaucratic channels. Philippe d'Iribarne was surprised that US workers thought an open door policy was normal when needed, though it was seldom used. By contrast, d'Iribarne found little expectation among French workers for easy communication across levels of the work hierarchy even though French workers recognized that more face-to-face communication would be more efficient.

Knocking On Doors

US Americans keep their office doors closed when they want privacy; those who wish to accept visitors have an "open door" policy. When a US American wants to enter an office with a closed door, she customarily knocks and waits for permission to open the door and enter. In France, business associates who have tacit permission to enter an office without appointments knock on a closed door and then enter. French doors are always shut and there is no understanding that closing a door indicates only a wish for privacy. The knocking is a message that warns the occupant of an immediate entrance. In France, the knock is not a request to enter but an announcement of entering.

Paper Matters

It is important to put all agreements in writing because the French do not consider anything official that is not written. It is essential to keep one's word, and a reputation for verbal honesty and dependability is important, but a document is official. French speakers can get carried away with their eloquence and they will also talk more for effect rather than to deliver precise communication. Listeners should be able to differentiate verbal fireworks from pragmatic communication. Get everything written down. An *aide mémoire* ("reminder") or written summary of what had been discussed during a meeting is an accepted way of reminding participants what has been said.

A registered letter is legally binding and is more likely to be answered. French correspondents are likely to ignore written requests that they do not like unless they are sent by registered post. Fax messages are becoming more accepted, but there is no guarantee that a response will be any faster than a registered letter. If a matter is urgent, it is always better to communicate in person than by correspondence.

Almost alone in the world, US Americans use 8.5 x 11 inch paper for business purposes. Europeans use the A4 standard specification, which is taller and narrower by about one inch, with the result that European storage spaces do not easily accommodate US paper dimensions (French paper size also does not fit well in US filing systems). It is better to use European-style paper dimensions for all correspondence whenever possible. We suggest sending all correspondence from the United States to France (and Europe in general) in the A4 standard forms as a courtesy. Those in the USA who receive letters in A4 style often cut an inch off the bottom of the pages to better accommodate US filing sizes.

Well-educated French are required to enroll in two foreign language programs before beginning their university studies. In Europe, and in France in particular, children are taught the basics of foreign languages before graduation from high school; universities do not teach beginning language courses, and college-level language classes are almost totally conducted in the foreign language. Most French children destined to attend universities are also sent to live in foreign countries for short stays to be immersed in languages. French multinational corporations sponsor language programs for their employees as a matter of course. As a result, most French businesspersons are familiar with English as a written language. It is common especially for older French to be able to write well in English using proper grammar, though not everyone will be familiar with idioms. But those who can write perfect letters in English may not be fluent in conversations. Anglophones find that many French are less comfortable speaking English than writing it. Do not assume that a French correspondent can speak English as easily as he writes it.

In addition, many higher-level managers receive translations of all correspondence and have language specialists draft all responses if necessary. It is easy, but mistaken, to assume that an exchange of letters in English indicates facility in speaking English on the part of the French author.

Finally, older, more conservative French executives do not feel completely at ease with e-mail. Internet messages often go unanswered or are delayed until an answer is necessary. Faxing messages, or overnight mail, are better means of communication than e-mail messages.

- Quote figures in euros and in metric

- French may let a foreigner struggle to speak French even if they speak English

- Do not force the French to admit they are mistaken

- The French do not respond well to "See this from my perspective"

❖   ❖   ❖   ❖   ❖

SUGGESTED READINGS

Barnes, Julian (2002) "Tour de France 2000," in *Something to Declare: Essays on France*. New York: Knopf.

Carroll, Raymonde (1987) *Cultural Misunderstandings: The French-American Experience*. Chicago, Illinois: the University of Chicago Press.

Foster, Dean Allen (1992) *Bargaining Across Borders: How to Negotiate Business Successfully Anywhere in the World*. New York: McGraw-Hill.

Victor, David A. (1992) *International Business Communication*. New York: HarperCollins Publishers Inc.

Wylie, Laurence and Rick Stafford (1977) *Beaux Gestes: A Guide to French Body Talk*. New York: The Undergraduate Press.

3

THE FRENCH WORLD OF BUSINESS

"System D" and "Le Cas Particulier"

The authoritarian part of the French national character encourages enactment of rules and regulations, while French individualism encourages the avoidance of rules. Foreigners find this contradiction both frustrating and confusing. However, this mix of individualism and authoritarianism is a central French national trait. The multinational stereotype below offers great insight into the French national character:

> In Britain, everything is allowed unless it is forbidden.
> In Germany, everything is forbidden unless it is allowed.
> In France, everything is allowed even if it is forbidden.

The result of this contradiction is "*système D*" ("system D"). The "D" is short for *se débrouiller*, "to make do, to untangle, to manage on one's own," as well as being resourceful in evading rules (or "*contourner la loi*," or getting around the law). The assumption is that laws are obstacles to be avoided. The French take great pride in getting around regulations to avoid bureaucratic red tape and gain some personal advantage over "them," or bureaucrats.

The most effective French executive is one who allows his subordinates to violate the rules when doing so increases efficiency. Philippe d'Iribarne observed engineers in a French factory making copies of keys to a relay station that they were forbidden to enter. The engineers themselves replaced blown fuses in the relay station instead of waiting several hours until a maintenance crew appeared. Carrying out this repair was forbidden to the engineers, but they did not want to stop work to wait for maintenance crews. No one complained or officially noticed the violations, and production stoppages were kept to a minimum. This is the French system of occasionally avoiding the rules at its best.

Using System D is best accomplished through personal relationships: a functionary is willing to ignore rules as a personal favor, though the ignoring of the rules must have some rationale or else the violator is punished. Using initiative is best accomplished when all concerned tacitly agree to an unauthorized course of action. This forces French managers who would otherwise be in competition with each other to form alliances for mutual protection when rules inhibit efficiency. Ignoring the rules is also impossible without the help of colleagues and others, so the individualism of French officials forces them to cooperate and develop extensive networks.

French managers extend this stance to everyone they work with. Foreigners who wish to conduct business with French decision-makers are forced to form alliances on the basis of trust and sociability. In France, business dealings remain very personal and no one will be effective unless she is diplomatic and able to convince French decision-makers that a proposal is one they wish to adopt even if success is based on violating some rules.

Philippe d'Iribarne (1989), after intensely studying a French factory, found that rules did not foster much cooperation. In fact, there was much competition among managers to see who would find the best solutions and who could extend their responsibility the most. Efficiency was achieved through personal contact: a positive personal relationship of one individual with another was the most singular manner of achieving a high level of cooperation among professionals. Foreigners wishing to get things done in France must adopt the French practice of also developing personal contacts.

Another central French characteristic is that, since rules are meant to be bent for the sake of efficiency, the French do not depend on rules and regulations as much as do Anglo-Saxons. US Americans, for example, assume that everyone should follow the rules and they become more upset when someone doesn't follow correct procedures. By contrast, the French assume that violators may have a legitimate reason for ignoring the rules. If there is disagreement on whether a rule has been ignored without good cause, the participants negotiate and the action is either accepted or the actor is punished informally.

By contrast, US Americans are more likely to seek redress from the courts or a higher authority to punish non-conformists. As a result, there is less reliance on the courts in France: disputes are more likely to be settled quietly and informally, as they are in Japan. Doing business in France necessitates developing a large network of supporters willing to defend the foreigner's cause and ignore rules for the sake of efficiency.

"*Le cas particulier*" refers to "special cases" or exceptions. This does not mean that flouting the law or a regulation is condoned, since France has been a legalistic country for centuries. Instead, potential offenders defend themselves by giving reasons why they acted in violation of the rules. A driver who speeds to take his pregnant wife to the hospital would argue, probably successfully, to the police officer who stopped him that driving over the speed limit to the hospital in this case was reasonable. It helps if the reason for bending the rules has an element of humor with it.

French respect general principles, but they also assume that principles should often be sacrificed for expediency. They assume that a rule, no matter how abstract or well constructed, always has exceptions. All rules, according to French thought, must be interpreted, and sometimes ignored because they are always limited. Rules serve people rather than the reverse. Decision-makers in France are taught the fine distinction of being flexible while still respecting the rule of law. Leaders are expected to be both law-abiding while enforcing rules case by case. They are flexible situationalists as well as legalists.

A consequence of this complexity is that French decision-makers find it possible to avoid rules when they wish. They are capable of denying a request because "it is against the rules" but finding that an exception is possible for a friend. The French are legalistic but remain flexible and ready to avoid rules on a case-by-case basis. This makes the French hard to understand, and causes great frustration among those foreigners who deal with the French.

This French predisposition to both make and ignore rules is different from the US American perspective. Americans feel that rules inhibit and that it's better to have as few rules as possible. Those rules that exist then apply equally to everyone. To Americans, rules provide for a "level playing field" so it is hard to see exceptions as anything but an unfair advantage. By contrast, the French attitude is that rules are necessary to avoid chaos. One can never predict reality completely, and while it is good to have many rules, it is also necessary to know when they can be ignored or bent a little. Finding loopholes and bending the rules increases efficiency, and makes work more interesting by allowing for individuality. A Belgian corporate director once compared French and German attitudes toward rules and regulations by noting that (Hill, 1994: 210), "The Germans say 'that's not possible here because of the law' when the first thought of the French…is 'that's the law, how can be get around it?'"

Historically, the pre-modern French legal system was developed to keep people from doing something (poaching, stealing, etc.) or to give advantages to friends of the powerful, such as giving royal favorites national monopolies. For most French, the legal system was seen as an oppressive system. Even today, under the current Napoleonic Legal Code now in effect, individuals are defined as guilty until they are proven innocent. It the responsibility of those arrested to show their innocence.

It is also necessary to look for legal loopholes. A law enacted on July 29, 1881, states that property owners are allowed to put notices on their walls stating that it is forbidden to place notices on the walls (*défense d'afficher*). But since the law mentions walls but not drainpipes, drainpipes in France are covered with advertising!

This search for loopholes is one of the major reasons why French society and its economy are dynamic rather than too bureaucratically rigid in the fashion of nineteenth-century China. This lack of respect for rules encourages French workers to be efficient. Japanese workers are efficient because they conform to group expectations, while French workers are efficient because they are willing to ignore rules if a goal can better be achieved by self-determination. We characterize French workers as being willing (when they wish) to go beyond the rules when necessary. This attitude is expressed by ingenuity in finding ways to "get around" the rules to achieve a goal.

Hair-splitting in France is extensively done today and is an old tradition. In 1765, a grocer named Boulanger began selling broth as a health product. He called his broths *restorants* (or restoratives). He later expanded his products by selling sheep trotters in a white sauce. However, since he wasn't a member of the stew sellers' (*traiteurs*) guild, he was sued by the guild. Eventually, Parliament voted to allow the sale of Boulanger's meats because it was decided that since they were not cooked in their own sauces, they could not be defined as stews and therefore did not violate the stew sellers' monopoly.

At its best, this French predisposition toward independent action allows workers to interpret the limit of their responsibilities and to extend these responsibilities without causing conflict. There is less likelihood in France than in China or Japan that workers will follow directives that they know are counter-productive. French workers, under the best scenario, are encouraged to use their initiative for the common good. Some workers, of course, can and will use rules to avoid innovation by "playing it safe."

French workers are highly productive when they wish to help the common good. When talking about their work, French workers say, "my work" and "my job." They feel bound, according to d'Iribarne, by a sense of honor to fulfill their work responsibilities. On the other hand, French workers can be very ineffective when they wish. They rely on rules to avoid contributions and their individualism can create pockets of non-cooperation throughout a company. Motivating French workers is a process of encouraging initiative within the rules. This is done in large part by making a project a worker's sole responsibility. This sense of responsibility is more important to the French than liking the work itself. French workers are quite capable of performing very dull and exacting work when they feel they are responsible for the project's success. Feeling in control is often more important than considerations of what one is accomplishing, if anything.

US American managers are more concerned with workers' morale than are French managers. French managers are more concerned with seeing that rules are followed, even if these rules inhibit efficiency. By contrast, US managers feel responsible for workers' satisfaction and self-achievement. They have more latitude in their work style. As a French factory manager commented, "the desire to please a supervisor is more developed (in the United States) than in France" because both foremen and line workers "negotiate" workers' treatment (d'Iribarne, 1989: 142).

American foremen and supervisors hope that production can be increased by increasing workers' personal satisfactions at work. Sociologist d'Iribarne found that American factory workers were more concerned that their supervisors act in a *fair* and *personal* manner; they also preferred being treated informally with a give-and-take attitude appropriate to various situations. By contrast, French factory workers preferred supervisors who followed established procedures and maintained more formal relationships.

French workers also received less praise than did American workers. French managers expected workers to follow orders in the same way they followed formal procedures. Praise is unnecessary when a worker does only what he is told to do. Supervisors react more to faults than to good work, which tends to be ignored.

Leadership

French leaders follow a paradoxical mix of autocratic and participative styles of leadership. They are autocratic because their positions and rank give them the right to give orders; they expect subordinates to follow orders. Since French workplaces have many rules, leaders are restricted in their autonomy but are also given the right to order workers as long as the rules are not violated. In addition, those with authority want to use their authority so that others recognize their higher ranks. French administrators and functionaries at all administrative levels can be capricious ("we will do this because I want it to be done"), especially when they feel their dignity is threatened.

On the other hand, subordinates are also protected by the rules and regulations governing their positions, and they also value whatever autonomy the rules give them. Leaders have to establish personal relations (within a formal setting) with subordinates or else the latter decrease their cooperation to the minimum required by the rules. French leaders become participative rather than authoritarian by necessity. They establish personal relationships with subordinates so that they develop enough personal loyalty to accept the legitimacy of superiors.

French leaders realize that authority is questioned by ordinary citizens and that resistance to authority is part of the French character. French subordinates for their part are likely to feel that authoritarian structures are necessary for others but not for themselves. Note the lack of degree of agreement in the positive responses of French and US American managers to the following two statements (Inzerilli and Laurent, 1983: 104); the French reflect a much more authoritarian attitude:

PERCENTAGE AGREEMENT TO THE FOLLOWING STATEMENTS

	FRANCE	USA
• No organization could ever function without a hierarchy of authority	73%	50%
• One should submit to all of a superior's demands if he has legitimate authority	19%	10%

Almost three-fourths of French managers accept the need for corporate leadership structures; the US American response was evenly split. US Americans are much less tolerant of leadership and, other studies indicate, of strict supervision. These attitudes are reflected in the US American ideals of self-employment and entrepreneurship. These values are much less prevalent among French employees.

A minority was more likely to say that a superior should be obeyed. The French proportion supporting the second question was twice as large as for the US American response, but a large majority of both national samples indicated a value for independence. French managers reserve the right to ignore superiors' directions, as do US American managers when they feel the directions are dysfunctional. Both national groups hold very similar values that the authority of superiors should be limited.

This attitude encourages French managers to negotiate constantly which rules are to be followed and how they are to be followed, and French organizational behavior is in large part the result of negotiation among colleagues. Middle-level managers are capable of deciding among themselves how to complete a project or even whether to innovate. The French system of management is more flexible than outsiders suppose.

French managers assume that all issues discussed with non-French are negotiable since they continuously negotiate among themselves.

This stance demands that outsiders develop skill in negotiation in order to convince French decision makers to accept their proposals. This usually demands the establishment of personal relations so that French managers feel inclined to convince their colleagues that a proposal is worth the effort of convincing others. It is not enough to present a good empirical case why a project should be accepted. It is also necessary to convince a French decision maker that a project is desirable enough for him to make the effort to convince others.

This French practice of constantly negotiating policy and procedures sharpens their negotiating skills, and French executives enjoy using these skills. In addition, French negotiating skills are based in part on extensive knowledge of what is being debated. While style and oratory are important, French leaders are also extremely well prepared to debate the objective merit of a proposal (or they wouldn't have become leaders) with anyone, even superiors. The French manager's prestige is based not only on his rank and position, but also how well he presents his arguments. It is also necessary for outsiders to be extremely well prepared to present their proposal with skill.

French leaders are also paternalistic in that they assume they are obligated to help those with lower status to a degree that would be unacceptable to US Americans. French managers are more likely to see themselves as having the responsibility to help others rather than allowing others to help themselves; the ethic of *noblesse oblige* is alive and well in France. Groups of European managers were asked to agree with one of the following statements, "It is obvious that if one has as much freedom as possible…the quality of one's life will improve…" or, "If the individual is continually taking care of his fellow men, the quality of life for all of us will improve, even if it obstructs individual freedom…" Selection of the first statement indicates the view that individuals should have the freedom to seek their own improvements in their quality of life as they see fit.

Below are the percentages of a number of national groups that selected the second statement indicating a preference for paternalistic leaders who feel obligated to control subordinates for their own good (Hampden-Turner and Trompenaars, 1993: 340):

Canada	80%	Sweden	61%
USA	**78%**	Italy	55%
Spain	70%	Germany	53%
Holland	70%	**France**	**45%**
Britain	68%		

French managers were most likely to reject the idea that personal freedom is better than direction by those in authority. North Americans (Canadians and US Americans) were the most (four out of five) individualistic in the degree of acceptance of this view.

French decision makers tend to see decisions as tentative and changeable. Unlike Japanese decision makers, French executives seldom feel bound by a group's policy. They can be convinced that a policy needs to be changed, and they do not feel obligated to follow established policy blindly. Although conservative, French leaders are capable of changing policy at a moment's notice, if only to express their individuality.

French leaders also expect subordinates to present them with compelling arguments detailing why a policy needs to be changed. Since a change of policy can be seen as an individualistic way to improve a situation, leaders encourage their subordinates to present them with new alternatives. French leaders will generally make unilateral decisions, but they are willing to listen to well-prepared arguments.

French leaders are also willing to consult with one another and their subordinates. They pay careful attention to others' proposals, and French decision makers are expected to listen to others' arguments and to be willing to be convinced by their ideas, although final decisions are made solely by the leader. Those who have a reputation for not listening to "reason" and logic are seen as bad leaders, but, in the final analysis, all leaders are expected to make decisions.

Decision making in a French corporation follows a strict hierarchy. The *président-directeur-général* (PDG)—the equivalent of chairman, CEO, and managing director—makes the major, and many of the minor decisions. Subordinates may suggest a solution to a problem, but the final word is given by the PDG. It is therefore best to contact the highest-level person possible because higher-level personnel have more access to decision makers. In addition, issues will not have to travel as far up the hierarchy before they are decided upon if one contacts someone close to a decision maker in the first place.

Authority

The French view authority as absolute. Holders of authority have complete power within their jurisdiction. Power is narrowly defined and those with authority are limited by either the rules or by the interpretation of rules on the part of their superiors. Within their jurisdiction, however defined, position holders see their authority as unchallenged and "theirs." Authority should be clearly defined to avoid misinterpretation and conflict. Ideally, those in authority have precise answers based on their expertise and knowledge of the rules and regulations.

Workers seldom have their names posted where the public can view them because authority is seen as belonging to the office rather than to the individual. Decision-makers see themselves as functionaries impersonally following rules and procedures. On the other hand, anonymity allows functionaries and those in authority to use their power arbitrarily if they can. The functionary can always blame the system or established procedures for his questionable actions.

Many observers of French bureaucracies have noted this paradox of centralized power coupled with independent subordinates. French sociologist Michel Crozier, whose work *The Bureaucratic Phenomenon* (1964) remains a classic analysis of French administrative behavior, states that the paradox mentioned above has two general consequences. First, leaders cannot provide real leadership on a daily basis because subordinates are too independent and they resist direction from above.

Crozier finds that "although [leaders] are all-powerful because they are at the apex of the whole centralized system, they are made so weak by the pattern of resistance of the different isolated strata that they can use their power only in truly exceptional circumstances" (Crozier, 1964: 225). Leaders lead most easily and effectively when there is a sense of crisis that forces subordinates to accept new directions from superiors.

Second, leaders in France find it almost impossible to introduce change in their organizations unless all those affected by the proposed changes are in agreement. Subordinates and regulations prevent them from introducing new ideas and projects into organizations.

Further, Michel Crozier states (1964: 227) that "Frenchmen do not dislike change; they dislike disorder, conflict, everything that may bring uncontrolled relationships; they cannot move in ambiguous, potentially disruptive situations." While we disagree that the French do not completely "dislike change," the end result is that (1) a sense of crisis is necessary to introduce real change in French corporations and, (2) individuals must want to become change masters. Otherwise they will, as Crozier found, prolong the very stalemate they have developed in order to protect their autonomy from a potentially autocratic system.

Teamwork

French individualism discourages teamwork and cooperation unless the work is highly structured. Higher-level administrators were educated in a very competitive environment and this competitiveness is reinforced by hierarchical structures at work. Rules give office holders an authority that cannot be shared with other office holders. This precludes much cooperation or teamwork because cooperation is an implicit ceding of authority.

Since French workers are (Oudot and Gobert, 1984: 84) "motivated as much by the wish to gain power as by the desire to achieve business goals," rules are necessary to encourage cooperation. A major goal of French white-collar workers is to personalize their position and individualize their procedures as much as rules allow. Workers therefore cooperate more easily with their superiors than with colleagues, since they see the latter as competitors. Few workers would accept the authority of team leaders unless that authority is clearly defined.

Teamwork increases the opportunities for face-to-face confrontation since teams seldom have enough rules to avoid conflict among members. Michel Crozier notes that a fundamental French trait is a dislike of face-to-face confrontation. Organizations establish rules in part to define clearly individual responsibility and areas of authority that avoid potential conflict among ambitious and competitive personnel. Teamwork challenges this system of authority.

In addition, the French understand power as defining the limits of freedom and autonomy, which they jealously guard within their jurisdiction. Teamwork reduces members to powerless equals, and is therefore to be avoided. Workers will use rules to protect their autonomy and there are few mechanisms in French corporations for extensive teamwork. Working in teams is seen as a US American practice and remains rare among French workers. French business graduate education has only begun to emphasize the teaching of such skills.

In the same way, French workers have not accepted "Management by Objectives" (MBO) because discussion of what a worker should do demands too much cooperation and face-to-face consultation. French workers also expect top-down management and are not used to making decisions on what they are to do. Workers expect to be told what to do within rules that define their responsibilities. Teamwork destroys this style of management. French workers are also suspicious of MBO because they fear that MBO allows supervisors to ignore rules and infringe on their rights. Skilled workers in France have a tradition of excellent craftsmanship, and they take pride in their work. From their perspective, the best supervisor is one who assigns them work according to established rules and then allows them the autonomy to complete their tasks in their own way.

Instead of expecting French workers to work efficiently as members of teams, US American managers in France would do well to compartmentalize a project into well-defined sections and then allocate these parts. French organizations have strictly defined areas of responsibility appropriate to each worker and work teams remain groups of individuals who are allocated parts of a project based on each member's expertise.

Meetings

Meeting rooms in France are formal; there are few attempts to make offices and conference rooms seem friendly or informal. US Americans often decorate their offices as extensions of their homes. Their offices contain family photographs, photographs of leisure activities and hobbies, and comfortable decorations. Offices in France tend to be cramped and austere, though higher officials' desks and chairs may be antiques as a sign of their status and sophistication. Conference rooms are similarly on the austere side.

The French maintain more formality during business meetings than do US Americans. They expect more respect, though younger professionals and businesspersons are becoming more comfortable with informal behavior among themselves. It is best to maintain formality with the use of last names and titles. Address everyone as *monsieur* and *madame*. Older persons prefer being called by their titles, and titles should be used at least during introductions, when hands are being shaken, as in *Monsieur le Directeur*, or *Madame la Directrice*. The importance of titles in France is such that those who hold the highest position in French corporations (*Président-Directeur-Général*) hold that title for life, and they expect to be addressed by that title while retired. Social amenities are kept short and business begins as soon as introductions are made and there is less small talk during the first part of business meetings than in English-speaking countries. Business cards are usually exchanged after the meeting rather than at the start.

In the United States and Great Britain, meetings often begin with an offer of coffee or tea. French businesspersons do not offer others anything to drink during meetings because eating activities are kept apart from business affairs and the two seldom occur together.

The visitor shakes hands first with the one who is most senior in rank. The French seldom discuss private matters during formal business meetings. They also dislike being asked personal questions. It is customary, however, to start a meeting with a short talk welcoming everyone, formally greeting the senior members of the French team, and mentioning your hope for a successful meeting. It is permissible to make a small joke about the weather or current affairs, or mentioning how glad you are to be in France, if appropriate. Business presentations should begin at this point.

Unlike US Americans, Germans, and Japanese, French businesspersons do not like to follow agendas strictly. The French prefer more give-and-take during meetings to allow for more free-ranging discussions, the expressions of impromptu thoughts, and the play of ideas. During meetings French also interrupt one another as they investigate abstractions that may not be completely germane to the official agenda. They are also likely to interrupt and ask questions when something of interest has been said.

Japanese hold meetings when consensus has already been achieved and colleagues are brought together essentially to confirm decisions that have already been agreed (Alston, 1990). US Americans prefer meetings that allow for both agendas (though they are often ignored in the heat of the conversations) and open discussions that debate all possible scenarios. Open debates allow individuals to present the best defense for their positions. Meetings often last until an agreement has been achieved.

For the French, meetings allow for personal expression and debates. Higher officials make decisions after meetings end even if they haven't been present at any of the sessions. French participants in meetings see discussions as chess games where different ideas and scenarios are presented and evaluated. They seldom demand signs of agreement or acceptance during a meeting because decisions are usually made in secret by superiors too important to be present.

US Americans are more linear in their presentations. They like to present a set of details and expect indications of agreement or disagreement as ideas are presented. Once a point has been made, US Americans also go to the next topic. US Americans assess the value of a meeting according to how much agreement has been accomplished rather than how much was discussed. The French evaluate the productivity of a meeting according to how much information was *presented* rather than agreed to.

US Americans also are used to presenting a completed plan; all that needs to be done during a meeting is to agree on the whole. French participants prefer meetings in which different alternatives and scenarios are presented as if they are tentative. The French process takes more time and more work is accomplished outside of meetings than during meetings. It is therefore important that participants at meetings only present broad outlines of a plan, and that they be prepared to present alternatives if necessary. French participants resist being overwhelmed by details; they do not want to have to limit their discussions to only one set plan.

A note of caution is necessary here. French individuals like to argue, especially when disagreeing on general principles and impersonal topics, such as where to buy the best cheeses in town. However, they do not like face-to-face confrontations so common in the United States. Discussions are animated but not personally confrontational, though foreigners often define French arguments as personal attacks when they are not. Working relations are formal in France partly to limit personalizing potential disagreements. Social distance should be maintained at all times with French colleagues or else they will define informalities as insulting. The French emphasis on rank dictates formal behavior. Nothing is meant to be taken personally when a French superior issues orders or offers work-related criticisms.

- Discuss general principles and avoid details at first

- Hand out extensive facts and details to be studied later

- Become excited only when discussing general principles

- Never become personal

- Be patient and expect a slow decision-making period after discussions take place

- Don't ask for on-the-spot decisions; decisions are made in private

As a result, meetings may be animated but behavior is not informal because there is no assumption among French colleagues that they need to be friends to work well together. They work well together because it is their formal responsibility to cooperate.

English and US Americans tend to assume that friendliness and informality increase morale and therefore productivity. French workers reject this personal attitude. All meetings, even when a superior talks to a subordinate alone in his office, should be formal.

In addition to being formal situations, French business meetings are used to distribute information quickly and to explain decisions that have already been made. Since French managers and executives respect thinkers more than doers, meetings are often occasions for self-expression. Not being invited to attend a meeting means being left out of an information loop and is taken as a loss of prestige and managers are evaluated in terms of who attends the most important meetings. More time-conscious foreigners such as Germans, Scandinavians, and US Americans see French meetings as more ceremonial than productive, but it is important to attend meetings even if the decisions are made elsewhere by those who may or may not attend the sessions.

French managers and executives do not like to schedule far ahead. They feel that schedules limit a person and prefer more flexible arrangements. As a result, powerful decision-makers tend not to confirm a meeting's date until fairly close to the time of the meeting itself. Unlike Germans and US Americans, French executives schedule an event near its occurrence and frequently change timetables at the last minute. Since French executives like to work under pressure, they accept last-minute rearrangements of schedules as crises that must first be dealt with.

French private or executive secretaries seldom make appointments for executives. Executives keep their own schedule books and decisions for scheduling are not delegated to anyone else, including private secretaries. Except for those in government, secretaries in France are allowed relatively little authority in terms of arranging meetings.

Finally, meetings are seldom scheduled for the weekend or during the summer vacations months. French decision-makers seldom work during the weekend, and many leave for their country homes on Fridays and some do not return until Tuesday. While executives may frequently work until nine o'clock in the evening, weekends are reserved for family and leisure activities.

French managers resist the US American custom of scheduling business breakfasts and, though the custom of business breakfasts is beginning to be accepted in a very limited way, most executives reject the notion. Many French workers at all levels commute long distances using public transportation, and arriving in town for an early business breakfast is extremely inconvenient. It is best to avoid business breakfasts even when time is short. French executives would probably not hurry a decision just to accommodate a foreigner.

✦   ✦   ✦   ✦   ✦

HOW TO BEGIN A PRESENTATION

Japanese begin with an apology.
Germans begin with a historical analogy.
US Americans begin with a joke.
French begin with a mention of French culture.

✦   ✦   ✦   ✦   ✦

Business Cards

Business cards are exchanged frequently in France. They are considered part of a person's first impression and therefore should be of good quality. Cards should be bilingual if possible. While all French businesspersons under the age of fifty read English with at least some ease, French language cards are a courtesy they appreciate.

Business cards are exchanged after handshakes. The recipient of a card should study a card for several moments to show respect. A stylish card case is necessary to place one's own cards and others'. The French see the placing of another's card in a trouser pocket as a sign of disrespect.

The French Concept of Competition

The French do not consider being competitive a positive quality. The term "competition" is used in France to describe athletic contests and educational entrance examinations. It is seldom used within a business context except as criticism. The term in business is used to denote a ruthless concern for business and profit that is unappealing and unattractive. French literature contains many anti-heroes whose main character fault was a competitive trait. A negative characterization of US Americans by the French is "competitive Americans," and foreigners who appear too competitive are rejected. The French would rather be secure than competitive.

French sociologists writing about work seldom mention or deal with the concept of "competition." The rationale for a project that "This will give you an advantage over your competitor" is counterproductive. Nor would the French accept the ability to become more competitive as a valid rationale for corporate growth. Concern for competitiveness as well as profit should be muted and understated. The French are competitive, but they consider mentioning this fact to be insulting.

Letters and Correspondence

French correspondence is formal and a central aspect of business etiquette. The written word is respected, and while speech can be florid and exaggerated, written messages are taken seriously and more literally. Written messages are considered official and the authors may be legally responsible for their contents.

Business communication also expresses the extremely fine distinctions in the social relationships of the participants as well as the relative social status of the correspondents. The US American practice of ending business correspondence with a "Yours faithfully" or "Best regards" is considered impolite among French business correspondents.

French correspondence readers would also feel insulted if a stranger addressed them in too familiar a fashion. The quality of the paper and of the envelope, the signature, and how ideas are expressed are also all used to evaluate the social and personal characteristics of the writer. Even how the paper is folded reflects on the writer. Handwriting is still used in French companies to evaluate the acceptability of job applicants, and handwritten notes are judged on the basis of handwriting style as well as on content, literary style, quality of paper, correct spelling, and grammar. Having a "power signature" appropriate to one's rank is also an important factor in impression management. Always remember that the French prefer style over content, in all ways.

The importance of style in business communications encourages French correspondents to rely on formulas and models to express themselves. Business letters convey the relationship of the correspondents through the use of set phrases. Below are business letters endings that offer subtle messages:

- To a colleague: *Je vous prie de croire, Monsieur, à mes sentiments les meilleurs*

- To a colleague one disagrees with: *Recevez, Monsieur, mes salutations*

- To a client: *Nous vous prions de croire, Monsieur, à nos sentiments distingués*

- To a supplier: *Je vous prie de recevoir, Monsieur, l'expression de notre considération distinguée*

The difference between the first two letter closures is the degree of formality; the first is warmer in style; the second is colder in feeling and more abrupt. The third and fourth differ partly in the change from "*sentiments*" to "*considération*;" the latter is less personal and more socially distant. A superior sends a subordinate a closing sentence giving *l'expression de ma considération distinguée*; a superior receives the writer's *très haute considération*; an equal receives the lesser *haute considération*.

Business letters remain formal even when the correspondents are in conflict with one other, or even if the letter contains the rejection of a project. Jean-Louis Barsoux and Peter Lawrence (1990) state that formality in correspondence maintains anonymity as well as impersonality. Just as important to the French, correct form indicates knowledge of the rules of protocol. Proper form reflects the writer's education and sophistication.

Proper form also helps to avoid a level of informality that might be inappropriate or rejected by one of the parties. Formality may help avoid anger by making criticism and rejection more impersonal.

Generally, business letters contain bad news only at the last. A letter may contain apologies for delays in answering, a comment on how the proposal was carefully studied by the writer and colleagues, and then the final closing sentence *Il ne saurait être question d'apporter à cette demande une suite favorable* (i.e., "no"). There would be little hint before the closing sentence that the message was in any way negative unless one was sensitive to form rather than content.

Persuasion

The French acceptance of logic does not encourage a reliance on past experience. Since theory is more important than mere facts, French executives are more likely to rely on their feelings and knowledge (i.e., education) than experience, which they distrust. Few French decision-makers would be convinced by an argument that relied on "what worked before" or "we did it this way and were successful." It is better to base an argument on logic rather than on past success. Alain Peyrefitte (1976: 12), a former member of the *Académie Française*, criticizes the French for being more comfortable with pre-fabricated ideas than with claims that "something works." For the French, reality is less real than theory. This is an important aspect of French character since US Americans are more likely to respect facts than ideas; French and US Americans see the world differently, and each should form their arguments in the way the other nationality can accept.

SUGGESTED READINGS

Axtell, Roger E. (1994) *The Do's and Taboos of International Trade: A Small Business Primer*. New York: John Wiley & Sons.

Gillman, Bernard and Martin Verrel (1994) *Mastering French Business Vocabulary: A Thematic Approach.* Hauppauge, New York: Barron's.

Hill, Richard (1994) *EuroManagers & Martians.* Brussels: Europublications.

Mole, John (1996) *Mind Your Manners: Managing Business Cultures in Europe.* London: Nicholas Brealey.

Oudot, Simone (1985) *Guide to Correspondence in French: A Practical Guide to Social and Commercial Correspondence.* Chicago: Passport Books.

4
NEGOTIATION

The French exhibit a unique style of negotiating strategies and behaviors that often confuse non-French negotiators. Non-French list the French as the most irritating and frustrating national group to negotiate with, though Chinese and Russians are also disliked for their negotiating styles.

This frustration with French negotiating behavior is in large part the result of cultural ignorance due to culture shock. French negotiators become less threatening when their behavior is better understood.

As noted below, French negotiators are extremely aggressive and competitive. In general, as already noted, French social values do not encourage competitive behavior since one should be polite at all times. But overt competitive behavior is encouraged in the French in two situations: athletic contests and negotiations. Normally calm and polite French individuals are expected to become aggressive during negotiations (and as spectators to athletic contests). French values dictate that the winner of a negotiation is the one who is not only the most verbally skillful but also the most successfully competitive. Negotiations are one area where the hierarchical elements of French culture are expressed openly: there must be a "winner" who is by definition "better" than the party who compromises more. French negotiators often feel as if their self-esteem depends on others' accepting their point of view.

However, we stress that the aggressiveness of French negotiators so disliked by other national groups takes an impersonal form. French negotiators do not personally insult others, nor do they threaten. Aggressiveness takes the form of verbal and logical displays, and all parties are expected to display verbal fireworks. French aggressiveness is more of a rhetorical style than an expression of personal dislike. It is primarily the way French negotiate.

In addition, debate during negotiations should provoke conflicts. Debates are seen as ways of showing one's intellectual power and superior personality, so that usually quiet French adults can become very vocal and loud during a debate. Negotiators are expected to attack their opponents' ideas and presentations. Foreign negotiators should not take this aggressive behavior among French negotiators as personal attacks, but rather as strategies common in French negotiating behavior. French negotiators would be surprised that their negotiating behavior was taken in a personal manner.

French negotiators almost always prefer to negotiate in French, and they insist on using the French language when the negotiations take place in France. The French respect their language and feel that it is the best one to use for negotiations. In addition, the French use negotiations as an opportunity to debate and show off their rhetorical skills. Thus, except for those who are extremely proficient in a foreign language, French negotiators feel much more comfortable when negotiating in their native tongue. Even French negotiators fluent in their opponent's language will negotiate in French if possible because of their pride in the French language.

French negotiators remain formal throughout negotiations. US Americans tend to adopt a more relaxed attitude after negotiations begin, on the assumption that spending time together places negotiators in a more personal relationship. French negotiators remain formal throughout negotiations, and would feel insulted if their opposites used their first names and adopted more relaxed postures. Those from more egalitarian cultures believe that informality, including use of first names, indicates equality and positive feelings. By contrast, French negotiators interpret informality as disrespect.

Dress also should be formal, and remain so. Negotiators should not take off their coats or loosen their ties. Dressing stylishly is an important aspect of first and later impressions since proper attire marks the person as worthy of respect.

In the same way, US Americans are likely to use humor to ease tensions and to show friendship. French negotiators feel that humor is misplaced during negotiations unless it is used to make clever remarks, or when sarcasm and cynicism is used. Humor among French negotiators is not used to ease tension or gloss over a point of contention but rather to show off one's cleverness. They also define humor as indicating a lack of seriousness and interest in the discussion. It is better to avoid humor unless a personal relationship has already been established.

French negotiations are uniquely, as well as extremely, logical and well organized. This Cartesian approach is highly respected as an aid to thinking in the French educational system. Cartesian logic is deductive and one uses well-established, *a priori* philosophical principles as a starting point for any discussion or presentation of an argument. The presenter begins with what is known, usually in an abstract form, then reasons through to a conclusion. Discussion then proceeds in an orderly (i.e., logical) fashion in which one point or fact leads to the next in such a way that no other interpretation is logically possible.

These *a priori* principles are often well-recognized formulas learned in school and recognized as legitimate by all well educated French university graduates. French education still uses memorization of standard answers and questions; many arguments among French individuals follow these traditional patterns. This practice can result in very traditional thinking and encourages a rejection of new, innovative decisions. This practice also gives non-French negotiators the impression, often correct, that French negotiators are inflexible and unwilling to change their positions in the face of new data. The consequence of these French thinking patterns is a reluctance to accept new ideas and ways of looking at a problem. French leaders are aware of this conservative tendency but find it difficult to change this practice.

Though French decision-makers are sometimes likely to use their intuition, they prefer deductive logic upon which to base their decisions. They remain very different from US American decision-makers and negotiators who prefer discussions based on relevant facts and who avoid deduction. Intuitive decisions will always be presented by the French as logical conclusions to a chain of logic when in fact they are not.

Another source of confusion for those dealing with French negotiators is the conception of time that is involved in negotiating strategies. French negotiators begin with a long-range view of how a specific proposal being negotiated fits into their company's long-term plans. Their mindset includes the place a proposal will affect other long-term policies. From their viewpoint, French negotiators are less concerned with short-term, specific consequences of their decisions. They therefore are more likely to include a larger range of issues in their negotiations that others nationalities see as irrelevant.

By contrast, negotiators from cultures more present-focused wish to negotiate issues that are specific and immediate. Long-term considerations tend to be rejected as irrelevant. US American negotiators are extremely present-oriented and tend to focus specifically on central issues on the agenda. They wish to consider only immediate issues to the exclusion of all else. US Americans are likely not to recognize why French negotiators seem to waste so much time on what to them are secondary or non-existent issues. Non-French negotiators should probe to discover all the issues that might influence an ultimate decision.

This feeling of confusion may be intensified by the difference between French and US American styles of discussion in general. The political scientist Stanley Hoffmann (a professor at Harvard University, but educated in France at a *grande école*) notes that in the US, differences are minimized at first. Discussion begins with what is already agreed upon, and important problems are left until the end. In France, however, it is the opposite: discussion often begins with what divides people (Hoffmann, 1977).

French negotiators seldom feel compelled to rush toward an agreement. They are willing to take as long as necessary to present their case and negotiate each point. French negotiators, like Japanese negotiators, believe that each point is as important as another. Unlike US Americans and British, French negotiators do not prioritize or rank issues in terms of their relative importance. They will spend as much time on a minor point as on a major one. This attitude tests the patience of national groups who are willing to gloss over minor points in order to speed toward an agreement.

French businesspersons have looser attitudes toward deadlines than those from Northern Europe and the United States of America. Non-French negotiators must learn to be patient. Negotiators may arrive late or cancel sessions at the last minute; they take time to study proposals very thoroughly, and the decision-making process is slow. French also do not like change, and time is spent placing new ideas within a more traditional framework.

The French higher educational systems teach the ability to solve problems of logic without the use of notes, when answering questions both in writing or verbally. A French negotiator may often discuss complex issues without looking at his notes. This is an impressive feat that can intimidate non-French negotiators. Such a custom may also extend negotiations when a French person repeats herself, or remembers a point that should have been made earlier. It is best to be patient with such behavior and resist the impulse to suggest something has already been discussed or is out of context.

Finally, French negotiators do not like to cede issues, nor do they like to compromise. Negotiation to the French is a zero-sum game in which one party loses when the other party wins. The concept of compromise is neither well developed nor accepted by French negotiators.

Negotiating Behaviors To Avoid

There are some behaviors that are inappropriate from the French perspective. Personal questions about family or work are considered invasive. Allow the French negotiators to be the first to volunteer private information about themselves. Presenting personal information is a sign of friendliness and acceptance, but the process should not be rushed.

French negotiators are, compared to many other national groups, blunt and direct. It is best to follow this practice and say directly (but calmly) what makes you unhappy about the negotiations. French negotiators expect others to be as frank and open about issues as they are. The French in general like persons who can defend their opinions. There is no need to be indirect, as one would be with Japanese negotiators, about expressing disagreements (Alston, 1990). One should, however, explain thoroughly why a disagreement exists. The French excuse almost anything except sloppy thinking.

However, French negotiators, while they accept passion in a discussion, do not respect anyone who loses his temper. The French see shouting and making empty threats as juvenile behavior. A combination of passion and logic is ideal; fist pounding and red-faced anger are counterproductive.

French negotiators do not expect to become close friends with their counterparts. They do enjoy eating good meals and good conversation with fellow negotiators, but friendship is usually reserved for non-business acquaintances. Acceptable openers to achieve more personal relations are to ask for information on local historical sights and restaurants. Mentioning that you are looking for the best place to eat seafood or drink the local wines, for example, will always initiate a good discussion.

Meals can be used as part of the negotiating process. Avoiding business-related conversations is appreciated during the first courses though formality is relaxed a little during the meal (but not completely; the French are there to enjoy a good meal and good conversation, not to become friends). Even long (two hours or more) meals are important parts of negotiations and should be enjoyed. Invitations to eat together should always be accepted. Meals are occasions when one can show off one's knowledge of French culture and show appreciation for the French way of living.

US Americans tend to "sell themselves" as part of their negotiating strategy. This approach repulses French negotiators; they feel that such aggressiveness suggests arrogance and boorishness. Behavior, posture, and dress should be low-key and formal at all times.

French negotiators do not appreciate displays of anger and raised voices. A common US strategy is to express anger and other emotions such as dismay and disbelief. Such emotionality is completely rejected by the French. French negotiators will not be swayed by emotional displays of any type.

French negotiators find US American optimism and "can do" attitudes irritating since life to the French is full of problems and as a result they tend toward pessimism. Pessimism and cynicism about current events are the norm among educated French adults. It is a bad strategy to make optimistic statements since French negotiators will almost always distrust and disregard them. It is counterproductive to sugarcoat or mince words.

French Negotiating Behavior

The first stage of the negotiating process among French negotiators is to discuss general topics only partly related to the project being negotiated. French negotiators will discuss general economic and business trends, the need for accepting the proposal (if they are the initiators), and the market shares of the companies involved. There may be a short discussion of government policies and how they influence current markets.

French negotiators will then present data on the potential profits of the proposal and its benefits for the companies involved. However, profits at this stage refer more to general benefits. The French in general feel uncomfortable when discussing profits or financial details. They believe that too much concern for monetary issues is a sign of boorishness. There will also be mention of the need for more unity among foreign companies. The French feel that it is important first to set the stage for the later negotiations and to mention how possible agreement will influence the companies.

The proper response for the visiting foreign negotiators is to present a long introduction, including the pleasure of being in France and dealing with those present. The formal atmosphere will begin to thaw at this point if the negotiator can be witty and show an appreciation of French culture and practices. It is also expected etiquette to mention the chief officers involved by name and show appreciation for the other company's hierarchy. Messages of good will from one's superior and CEO are also highly appropriate at this time.

In addition to making direct references to profit, a serious gaffe at this point is to suggest that an agreement needs to be achieved quickly. The mention of both money and time limitations during this preliminary stage would make the French negotiators lose respect for their counterparts. The more impatience is shown the less likely the negotiation will be to succeed. French negotiators and their superiors do not like to be rushed. They feel that being rushed is a strategy to force them to make inappropriate concessions. It is imperative not to establish any deadlines during this or any other stage of the negotiation.

French negotiators are also likely to mention the close relations and friendships of the companies and personnel involved. These are set phrases that have no relation to the eventual outcome of the negotiations.

Below is a table adapted from John Graham's (1996: 82) experiments in simulated negotiating sessions that measure three aspects of negotiating behavior using French, German, US American, Mexican, and Japanese participants. (1) The number of times "no" is said indicates the degree a national group is willing to reject their counterparts' proposals as well as a willingness to express conflict opinions openly.

(2) The number of interruptions indicates a certain aggressiveness and willingness to control the negotiations. (3) Using the term "you" indicates possible disagreement and indicates a psychological separation of one speaker from negotiation opponents. By contrast, using the term "we" indicates possible agreement and a willingness to cooperate.

✦   ✦   ✦   ✦   ✦

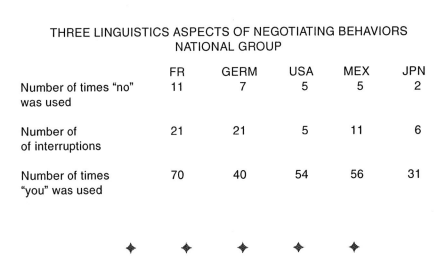

THREE LINGUISTICS ASPECTS OF NEGOTIATING BEHAVIORS
NATIONAL GROUP

	FR	GERM	USA	MEX	JPN
Number of times "no" was used	11	7	5	5	2
Number of of interruptions	21	21	5	11	6
Number of times "you" was used	70	40	54	56	31

✦   ✦   ✦   ✦   ✦

French negotiators are more likely than any of the national groups in the table above (or any other national group) to say "no," in part because they enjoy arguing for its own sake. The ability to debate and discuss an issue with elegance and style is a mark of a well-educated person, and the practice of rhetoric remains a well-respected ability in France. A good discussion from the French perspective demands disagreement, which in turn demands constant "no's" to indicate that disagreement. Constant agreement, on the other hand, suggests subordination and inferior knowledge: one who agrees must have little to say.

In negotiations, agreement also suggests that a negotiator has presented such a good argument that further debate is unnecessary. Agreement also ends a possibly enjoyable discussion. Since style is often preferred to fact during a discussion, French negotiators can become carried away and resist agreement just because they enjoy continuing a good argument.

In the same manner, constant agreement subordinates one's individualism to the one who talks more. Agreement indicates conformity that in turn encourages French negotiators to argue almost for its own sake. Dean Allen Foster (1992: 90-2) points out that French individualism is defined when a person is *in opposition* to another person's ideas. US Americans are also open about their views, but American negotiators are more likely to declare their position without arguing the issue or attacking their opponents' presentations. Americans are more likely to defend their position than attack others' presentations. For the French, opposing another's ideas is open-ended and unlimited, and demands as much discussion as is needed to present one's case fully. The concept of debate includes the element of criticizing others as well as presenting one's case.

French negotiators do not take other persons' "no's" personally. A "no" is merely an expression of individuality and is not seen as an attack on the other person. Responding with a "no" and taking part in another's argument is also seen as showing interest and respect for what is being said. Disagreement in this context is an indication of respect that the speaker has said something worth disagreeing with. By the same token, French negotiators accept "no's" from others and do not see them as insulting.

French negotiators have a reputation for ending negotiations and leaving the negotiating table when they find themselves losing an argument. They are likely to leave the debates and declare themselves at such a complete impasse that further negotiations would be useless. The fact that the French negotiators are talking, even if only to say "no," means they wish to take part in the negotiations and is thus a positive sign.

The table above also indicates that French negotiators are most likely to interrupt their foreign counterparts. As with a "no," interruptions are understood by the French as engagement and interest, rather than as insults or as an unwillingness to talk only when it is one's turn. French speech patterns follow overlapping patterns, as speakers interrupt each other in their haste to present their views. US American speech patterns follow a more linear pattern, as the listener waits until the speaker has completed a full thought before taking a turn (Carroll, 1988).

However, US Americans, in their haste to complete a thought and to take their turn at speaking, often finish another's sentences. The French feel this habit of sentence-completion is insulting as well as rude. It assumes the speaker is so simple that the other person realizes what will be said next. When negotiating with the French, US Americans and other national groups that exhibit similar speech patterns should force themselves to interrupt more often and also to avoid ending each other's sentences.

A very disturbing practice of French negotiators is the tendency to interrupt their opponents' opening statements. Non-French may see this as an unwillingness to listen even when negotiations have barely begun and when there is as yet no specific proposal to discuss. French negotiators interrupt opening statements to ask questions because they are attracted to something that has been said and they wish to add a comment. Since French negotiators place greater importance on the beginning of negotiations than the following parts, they listen to opening statements more carefully than do other national groups. They also enjoy debating and want to join in the discussion as early as possible.

The solution is to see interruptions during this first, introductory, stage as interest on the part of the French negotiators. They also want to control the framework of later negotiations by establishing their views as early as possible. Non-French negotiators should accept these interruptions even when little specific content is being presented.

These interruptions will end shortly and the presenter can continue as planned.

French negotiators also use the term "you" most often. This speech pattern is a reflection of the fact that good arguments and one's sense of individuality demand opposition. The French also say "you" often because they are trying to control the negotiations by re-defining an ongoing argument to their own advantage. It is a strategy that enables the speaker to dominate an argument. This word usage is also a reflection that French negotiators do not think in terms of a more cooperative "we."

The Negotiation Process

French negotiating strategy is first to develop the framework for the debate. They prefer establishing general principles that provide guidelines for the negotiation itself. This concern for the establishment of general principles forces French negotiators to prepare their strategy and opening arguments very carefully. French negotiators see the negotiating process as a problem of logic that convinces others that their arguments are too rationally constructed to be denied. They are prepared to answer logically their counterparts' own logical structure when it is presented. The establishing of a set of general principles to guide negotiation is a way of controlling events and avoiding uncertainty. French negotiators like to feel as if the negotiation process is controlled and predictable.

This approach differs from that of US Americans, who tend to see negotiations as a poker game where each position is kept hidden until the last minute. In addition, US Americans customarily begin negotiations by presenting a series of detailed points, each of which should be decided upon in sequence. US Americans like to solve directly points they feel are the most contentious. To them, the negotiation process is a series of issues to be settled by compromise.

By contrast, French negotiators present well-prepared and logically arranged positions that announce clearly what they want to achieve from the negotiations. They are not prepared to discard their first position and adopt other scenarios. Any possible compromise means that the original position has to be rejected and a new proposal developed. This lack of preparation for possible compromises causes delays in achieving a final solution and gives the impression that the French are too arrogant to compromise. The French will compromise, if necessary, but such compromises are not implicit in their beginning strategies.

French negotiators feel that the best way to solve a problem is to study it as much as possible. They then search for a solution after extensive study. By contrast, Northern Europeans and US Americans prefer to attack a problem immediately in successive stages. To them, intellectualizing a problem instead of searching for solutions is a waste of time.

Note that at this stage, French negotiators see factual presentations as irrelevant and unconvincing. Facts enter the discussion after the logical arguments unfold. The first stage of negotiation is the presentation of a logical argument based on general principles rather than on empirical presentations. Remember that to the French, logic is more convincing than facts, and French negotiators pay attention to factual arguments only during the later stages of the negotiation. The presentation of facts during these first stages of negotiation is seen by the French as a hard-sell tactic, which they reject as being too aggressive. They see factual presentation as an opponent's strategy of distraction because their own arguments are failing.

This strategy also allows them to control the negotiations on the assumption that no new information that falls outside the established general principles can be introduced after they have been established as the ground rules for negotiation. Doing so disturbs French negotiators since they do not like to feel unprepared.

Negotiating Strategies

French officials and decision makers, including negotiators, respond better when they feel they have achieved rapport with their negotiating counterparts. Otherwise they will remain formal and aloof. The best means of establishing rapport is to dine together. While many French executives play golf or engage in other sporting activities such as boating or tennis, the easiest way to become friends is over a good meal with good conversation. The non-French negotiating team should host several lunches at better restaurants to break down the wall of formality the French erect when dealing with strangers. In addition, members of the negotiating team should individually invite their counterparts for meals and other activities. While business is seldom discussed during meals, a few comments over the cheese and dessert courses can be presented to clarify selected points that are being negotiated.

French negotiators are seldom in a hurry to complete negotiations. They enjoy debates and presentations, and they are hesitant to hurry an agreement for fear they have not gained the most advantage possible. French decision makers believe that important decisions should be carefully studied. A negotiator who implies to the French that there is a need for a quick decision has lost an advantage. The French will merely slow down the pace of negotiators in the hope that delays will gain them some advantage.

A challenge when negotiating with the French is the necessity of being understood. The French conversational style includes body language and gestures that are specific to French culture. French negotiators use head gestures and facial expressions to indicate agreement and disagreement. A pursing of the lips accompanied with a slight frown means either disagreement or that the listener does not completely follow the speaker's argument, for example.

Although French negotiators seem very aggressive to other national groups, they nevertheless enjoy a limited amount of humor during negotiations. French humor tends toward making clever cynical remarks and allusions; in that way French humor is similar to the US

American style of humor. A French negotiator may make seemingly bitter remarks. Such remarks are intended to be more humorous than aggressive and should be taken as signs of friendship: only friends would make fun of "the system" or groups of people (say accountants or engineers) during negotiations. A French negotiator might state that "Accountants always ruin good agreement," or "Who can predict what French government officials will do to the strength of the euro?" These comments are most likely signs of friendliness rather than hints that an agreement is too vague or that more guarantees of currency support are needed.

While humor can mask strong objections to a specific part of a proposal, humor is more likely to be only pleasant conversation. Humor indicates that a business acquaintance is relaxed enough with you that a humorous comment is acceptable. However, while humor expresses the health of a relationship, it does not signify any relaxation of negotiation alertness or any willingness to compromise.

French negotiators find it difficult to admit they have not understood a presentation or part of an argument. A useful strategy to use with French negotiators is to ask "Have I been clear enough?" This query places the burden of possible lack of clarity on the speaker rather than the listener and gives a face-saving opportunity to ask questions. Another useful strategy is to repeat important segments of a presentation in slightly different forms.

However, French negotiators, if their opposites are speaking in English, are likely to withhold their questions until they can analyze the empirical and technical material at their leisure. Under such circumstances, it is best to accept a slower pace of negotiations while the members of the French team re-group and discuss among themselves what has already been presented.

French negotiators may not be familiar with US Americans' use of sport idioms, general slang, and selected gestures, and presentations should be prepared with this in mind. Offering the suggestion that an idea comes "out of left field" will be baffling to French listeners and likely be misunderstood. Making a circle with thumb and first finger signifies agreement to Americans but is defined by French as "nothing" or worse. A shrug by a French individual means mild disagreement, disbelief or, less frequently, disdain. A shrug also can mean the listener is withholding a comment or evaluation.

In summary, French negotiators respect verbal presentations more than technical presentations. Style is more important than content during the active phases of negotiations. French negotiators will pore over all technical data at their leisure, and presentations should be more verbally coherent than technical. In fact, French negotiators tend to feel that numerous overhead transparencies and presentations of technical data during negotiations are likely to hide a weak argument and a lack of substance. Verbal presentations should be tightly structured and elegant; technical data should be presented almost as an afterthought.

French decision makers tend to rely on their subordinates for evaluations of technical data. Leaders prefer to concern themselves with the "big picture" and let others pore over technical details. French negotiators will, as a result, become bored with an overly-technical presentation and feel that such an argument is *de facto* inadequate. On the other hand, negotiators must present as much technical information as possible in written form and allude to rather than describe it during the negotiating sessions.

While French negotiators expect other national groups to negotiate in French, at least while in France, they are not likely to remember to be considerate and speak slowly and clearly. Talk will often become more rapid as negotiation progresses and the French negotiators become engrossed in the discussions. It is very useful to have as part of the negotiating team one or more members who are fluent in French.

Negotiating decisions are seldom made unilaterally by the members of the French negotiating team. Since even authoritative leaders are accustomed to discuss potential decisions with subordinates and their peers, decision makers do not like to make on-the-spot decisions. They will consult with as many persons as they feel are necessary. Consultation is not seen as a weakness by French leaders, though the one who makes unilateral decisions *after consultation* is respected. This need for extensive consultation takes time and delays making a final decision.

French negotiators almost always listen carefully to all arguments and presentations. The leader will then thank the opposite negotiators for an excellent presentation and will, most likely, offer a positive reaction to the presentations. A common concluding set of comments is to state that the arguments presented were well constructed and organized, and that the proposal has great merit. The French representatives, however, are merely being courteous and no positive statement at this time should be taken at face value.

They will then say that they must discuss the matter with others, including their superiors. There may be some hints that difficulties still exist, but that it is hoped that a deal can be accomplished. Much of the discussion at this time is formal and means very little. Few French negotiators will make binding statements at this stage.

Agreements in France are not considered binding unless they are in a written form and signed by the responsible officials. Positive statements at the end of negotiations are verbal "noises" that mean very little. They are meant to express politeness rather than a decision, and US American negotiators should accept them as such.

SUGGESTED READINGS

Binnendijk, Hans (1987) *National Negotiating Styles*. Washington, DC: Department of State Publication, Foreign Service Institute.

Fisher, Glen (1980) *International Negotiation: A Cross-Cultural Perspective*. Chicago: Intercultural Press.

Moran, Robert T. and William G. Stripp (1991) *Successful International Business Negotiations*. Houston: Gulf Publishing.

Sheppard, Pamela and Bénédicte Lapeyre (1993) *Negotiate in French and English/Négocier en anglais comme en français*. London: Nicholas Brealey Publishing.

5
BUSINESS ETIQUETTE

Names And Titles

In the United States people like to pretend that class differences do not exist. This attitude encourages informal behavior on the assumption that informality implies equality. Similar to Australians and Israelis, US Americans are seen as almost aggressively informal by people throughout the world. A rule of thumb for US Americans engaged in international business is to be more formal than customary. Not doing so creates a very negative impression to those not used to US American informality. Most persons throughout the world equate formality with politeness and respect.

This informality manifests itself in the American practice of being on a first-name basis with almost everyone. US Americans commonly address letters and one another using first names, a practice almost unknown in most parts of the world. One of the most irritating aspects of dealing with US Americans, according to foreigners, is the informal use of first names. While ignoring titles and more formal forms of address implies friendliness and equality among US Americans, the French reaction ranges from irritation to insult.

The French are conscious of titles even in the most casual conversations such as greetings by a store clerk or even a neighbor. All adult women are given the title of "*madame*" irrespective of marital status ("*mademoiselle*" is limited to waitresses). A simple "hello" will almost always be followed by a title: "*Bonjour, monsieur;*" "*Bonjour, madame.*"

The person's title is added in business relationships to increase courtesies, such as "*monsieur le directeur*" or "*madame le ministre.*"

The protocols for proper gender titles in France are both complex and changing, and proper language usage is difficult for even native speakers. In some cases there are feminine forms of business titles, such as "*la directrice.*" But a number of professional titles do not have feminine forms or else are seen by the French as demeaning, as in "*la doctoresse,*" which is grammatically correct but taken as insulting.

To add to the confusion, some forms of address do not refer to the office holder at all! The title "*madame la ministre*" refers to the (male) minister's wife and not to a female minister. To address a female office holder, the safest strategy for the non-expert is to use the masculine form of the position with a feminine prefix such as "*madame le ministre.*"

In a study of French managers, the researchers found that two-thirds believed that a corporation is basically "a system of authority." French managers demand clear lines of authority, in part so that they know where their area of responsibility ends and another's begins (Gordon, 1996: 137). This is reflected in the French manager's emphasis on formality and respect based on rank and position. It is therefore extremely important to address French managers correctly by their formal titles. It is also important to recognize the chain of command and to offer senior persons more courtesies.

Informality is not encouraged among French managers since they believe this blurs the lines of authority and ignores the formal nature of the work environment. New employees in France are taught not to confuse the official with the personal. It is best to maintain a limited amount of formality and seriousness during business hours. Co-workers become more informal away from work.

Dress Codes

Proper dress is important when meeting business colleagues. Business dress is formal at all times, especially in the North and in Paris. French individualism leads the French to base their evaluations of others largely on first impressions; the French assume that they can immediately evaluate a person using their own instincts and personal sense of style. It is important to dress for success when dealing with French businesspersons, since the French place great emphasis on appearance and posture. Dress to the French indicates one's place in society; people are expected to wear more fashionably correct attire as they move up the social ladder.

Men generally wear dark suits at work; accessories should match. Women should wear modest fashions with stylish accessories. Businesswomen in France are also expected to be feminine and should not wear the equivalent of men's fashions. Current hairstyles and jewelry are expected. There should be no false modesty in dress and accessories when dealing with French businesspersons, but ostentation should also be avoided.

Military draftees in France traditionally wear blue shirts that will stand wear and tear better than dress shirts. A person who wears a blue shirt in a business context may be seen as *un bleu*, or novice.

In addition to general appearance, French take shoes seriously, and these should be fashionable and well polished. Wear the best shoes you have to business meetings. Doing otherwise may become a source of ridicule.

As with the use of titles, French culture is more formal than the United States in terms of dress code and general self-presentation in business. Although the business suit is less universally emphasized in France, certain minimum standards of "good taste" are still expected. Those who do not meet this minimum are seen as immature or, worse, lower class. The individual who is inappropriately dressed for business is viewed as ridiculous. These standards apply to both women and men.

Professionals such as engineers are allowed more leeway than businesspersons in their dress codes. For those who are not managers or executives but who hold more technical positions, a well-made jacket and tie (or even a more daring turtleneck) are acceptable alternatives to the more traditional suit and tie. Women can wear less formal alternatives than suits, but their dress should be fashionably appropriate for business.

The pitfall for many US Americans is that they may rely on expense instead of currently defined good taste as a guide to what they wear. French business individuals stress good taste and discretion above all. An Armani business suit, a silk shirt, and Italian shoes are acceptable in a business context if done discretely. The basic rules here are that eveningwear is not appropriate for business wear (this applies to both men and women) and that subtlety is preferred over cost.

Whether *haute couture* or off-the-rack (notice the first term is in French and the second in English), the guiding principle should be good taste rather ostentation. Good taste among French can be reduced to classic tailoring that is sober and discreet. Note that French business suit styles differ from US American and British styles, so that even if well-dressed, foreigners will still be seen as not quite dressed in the French style. This is acceptable as long as the fashions worn are discreet and formal.

The main exception to the guidelines above for members of Anglo-Saxon cultures (primarily the USA, Great Britain, Canada, and Australia) is that, in France, men traditionally wear brighter colors outside of business settings. Even within business contexts, French business attire has more colors, especially with accessories. The rule here is to achieve proper color coordination to evoke a sense of fashionable flair. In this context, men's ties become fashion statements. No one should ever wear a tie that is humorous or because, "My son gave me this tie." If you feel that you need to explain or apologize for why you are wearing a certain tie, it is better to not take it to France.

European fashions for all occasions are more formal than in the United States. "Casual wear" for sports or other activities are only casual in relation to work attire. Those expecting to play golf or tennis or go yachting are expected to wear the traditional clothing for those activities.

Business Lunches

When they were students, all French businesspersons over the age of about twenty-five were given two-hour lunch breaks from school so that they could go home to eat lunch. As adults they are used to stopping work around noon for a long lunch, and the habit dies hard. Younger French workers are less used to long lunch periods, but the lunch period still tends to be of great concern. For most French, the noon meal is the major meal of the day.

A common strategy among French managers is to hold meetings late in the mornings in the hope that the approaching noon hour will encourage someone to make ill-advised decisions in order to end the meeting for lunch. On the other hand, French negotiators may lose interest in business topics after eleven o'clock; they begin to worry about where and what to eat for lunch, and they begin to worry whether they will lose this personal time. Some may go home or to visit a lover for a few hours in the early afternoon and do not want to linger at the office as noon approaches. Presenters may lose their audience's attention if meetings do not end soon after 11:15 or so.

Japanese and US American middle-level and above managers customarily grab sandwiches to eat at their desks. What is eaten during these times is considered less important than how fast it can be consumed. This could not be less true among the French, and eating a fine lunch is seldom neglected because of work responsibilities. Negotiations with French associates are not possible without a series of meals to facilitate mutual understanding. As a French sales director noted "It not unknown for a meeting to be postponed for several weeks simply because of a failure to find a free lunch hour." (Barsoux and Lawrence, 1990: 106).

Accordingly, a business lunch should not be viewed merely as a way of getting work done. Approaching a business lunch in this simple way with French businesspersons becomes extremely counter-productive. The French will not want to do business with you if leisurely business lunches are not possible.

The business meal in France demands a number of adjustments for which foreigners are often ill prepared, but the meal itself is a central aspect of business in France. The first adjustment non-French must make when considering a business (or social) luncheon date is that the meal is a *formal* occasion and that personal enjoyment should be at the bottom of your list of priorities. As with all social occasions for the French, eating together means that every aspect of your self-presentation will be judged and evaluated. The ultimate success of the business deal hangs in large part on the impression you make during the meal. You must give the impression of being cultivated, able to converse intelligently and articulately, know the rules of dining etiquette and show both a knowledge and appreciation of good food and wine. Business lunches are serious matters with the French and remain more social than business-related. Generally, business is seldom discussed until near the end of the meal.

The second adjustment to be aware of is that French food servings tend to be smaller than those found in the United States, England, and other European countries. The French prefer quality, flavor, and variety to quantity. They ridicule the US American attraction for larger, simpler, and cheaper meals and critically call Americans "overfed Americans." They feel that an "all you can eat for $9.95" meal is unsophisticated and better offered to children. While the French enjoy guests who appreciate their food, they do not admire heavy eaters.

✦　　✦　　✦　　✦　　✦

PERCENT OF NATIONAL ADULT POPULATIONS
CONSIDERED OBESE

Australia	20.8%	Britain	21.0%
France	**9.6%**	Japan	2.9%
US	**26%**		

Source: *The Wall Street Journal*, 7-1-02.

The proper behavior is to accept smaller portions, eat a little of each dish, and refuse seconds. It is expected that you will eat everything on your plate (which is why, if you have the opportunity, you should take only a small portion). While it is common, and indeed even expected, for women in the US to leave about half of what they are served (for doing otherwise is to appear gluttonous in US American eyes), this is seen as wasteful and capricious by the French. A two or three-hour meal should be savored. For formal occasions, a banquet may last four to six hours; small portions are necessary for survival.

The third adjustment is to drink less during meals. The French drink less during meals than do US Americans. Even bottled water, which used to be expensive but necessary because of the once inadequate purity of the public water supply, is drunk sparingly. The foreign tourist who drinks large amounts of water is a figure of ridicule among the French. There will be asides about "American camels." US Americans going to France for the first time will be surprised by the fact that there are no drinking fountains in France. They do not exist at airports, near restrooms (toilettes), or movie theaters. Most public fountains have water that is drinkable (*eau potable*) and tourists can fill their bottles there. Wine in France is seldom drunk before a meal. A small glass of *apéritif* is common, but only one. The main activity is the meal, not pre-dinner activities.

The fourth adjustment deals with the behavior expected of diners during a meal. The importance of behaving in a "cultural" manner has already been discussed but cannot be underestimated. Meals are occasions to show one's social and cultural sophistication rather than to make serious business decisions.

Conversations during business meals should be light and impersonal. As Harriet Welty Rochefort puts it, "Outgoing Americans are generally disturbed when they go to dinner parties and realize they have to button up their mouths on almost every single subject that could reveal something personal about themselves. Otherwise the person next to them could think he's been mistaken for their therapist" (Rochefort, 1999: 45). If you want to know more about the personal life of others, you can start by casually saying something about your own life such as, "My wife/husband says…" or "I have a ten-year-old boy who likes xxx." The act of volunteering personal information in appropriate contexts is a signal to others that they too can ask personal questions or volunteer information themselves. They may take the opportunity to reciprocate with similar pieces of personal information, thereby also giving you the chance to ask follow-up questions. But go easy on asking for or giving out personal information. Do not show family photographs during a business meal. The French are less interested in your personal history than in enjoying a pleasant and witty conversation on subjects of interest to everyone.

The fifth adjustment non-French must make when considering business lunches is that meals reflect the host's prestige. The host gains prestige when he hosts a business meal in a gourmet restaurant, preferably one well known or one offering special dishes. Being recognized by the staff is a plus, as is being able to assume the bill will be sent to the host's company so that no money changes hands in front of guests.

The host also can control the eating session to gain psychological advantage. The hostess already has shown that her company and her taste are impeccable, and that she is recognized by the staff of an *haute cuisine* establishment. She then makes suggestions for what will be eaten based on whether she wants to present heavy dishes and much wine to cause a food-induced stupor among guests. French hosts are not above forcing too much wine on foreign guests to place them at a disadvantage.

French believe in the old adage "You are what you eat" and they judge others by the foods they serve. One of the authors' friends described a couple as follows: "Their lives are as dull as the cheeses they serve."

A last piece of advice is never be intimidated by a waiter. Establish eye contact with your waiter, say *Bonjour*, and ask what he recommends. You always (or almost always) will receive better treatment when you establish a personal relationship with waiters, clerks, or government officials. Saying a dish has been particularly good during a business meal pleases both the waiter and French diners; it is especially rewarding to tell the host that a meal was exceptional and well selected.

Now you have eaten a meal of several courses (appetizers, one or two meats, salad, and vegetables) and small amounts of bread during nearly the last two hours. (The salad course comes *after* the main course in France and not before as in the United States.) There have been several types of wine and witty conversation about history, culture, and current events.

It is now time for the cheese course followed by dessert and coffee. It is bad taste to take too much of the five to ten different cheeses being offered and never take a second helping. There may be a new wine to go with the cheeses. It is now time for desert. Then it's time for the coffee course, which is often served alone or after the meal proper has been completed. This may take another half hour. Coffee is never served throughout a meal and is never taken with milk or cream except at breakfast. You will also be offered a *digestif* such as cognac or different flavored liqueurs afterwards to help digestion. Only then is it proper to smoke.

It is permissible to begin business discussion when the cheese platter appears. It is not permissible to bring up business-related topics before then. If you have performed well up to this point, you will have won the confidence of your French associates. They will be ready to do business with someone they now think of as their own kind of person.

Superiors use the practice of hosting lunches as indications of favoritism. Subordinates taken out to lunch by their bosses feel flattered, especially when the meal is *haute cuisine* and long. Since business meals are primarily social affairs, eating with the boss indicates a closeness and informality not allowed in French offices. US Americans use the term 'to butter up' to indicate flattery; French superiors also know how to use food to the same advantage.

FOOD ANALOGIES IN BUSINESS

Les grosses légumes:	(big vegetables) top brass
Faire des choux:	(make cabbage) make profit
Bouffer de l'argent	(eat money) losing money
Tourner au vinaigre	(turn into vinegar) bad turn of events
Mettre de l'eau dans son vin	(water one's wine) compromise

Source: Barsoux and Lawrence, 1990: 105.

✦ ✦ ✦ ✦ ✦

We offer two final warnings when eating out in France. Diners do not take excess food home. There are no facilities for carrying food outside a restaurant. Eat all you wish and leave the rest. Asking to take food home is considered an insult, and is definitely not a French custom. Second, dog lovers often take their pets to cafés and restaurants. Most dogs in France are trained to lie close to their owners and are seldom in the way. It is best to watch where you step (as always, in France) as you are led to a table in order not to cause a disturbance by stepping on a dog's tail. The French do not view the presence of a dog as compromising hygiene, and may perceive it as yet another example of the American obsession with sterilizing nature if you make a fuss.

Personal Relations

As frequently noted earlier, the French see much of business as personal behavior within an office holder's area of responsibility, but this important point is worth stressing. That is, a French manager obeys the rules defining his responsibilities but expects to be allowed independence within these rules. One measure of this independence and individuality is to act according to personal whims whenever possible. As a result, it is important to develop and maintain personal relations with French counterparts. Being personally known to a manager opens doors strangers find closed. Effort has to be made to maintain personal relations through frequent dinners, after-sales calls, etc. The French seek alliances with fellow workers and anyone with whom they do business. Often, the best, and only, way to approach someone is through a personal introduction from a third person.

Humor

Humor (as distinct from wit) is seldom expressed during work or during formal occasions. Nor is humor used to make a point. Ideas and presentations are too respected to be based on humor. Humor at work is often defined as frivolous and inappropriate; joking may also be seen as an unwillingness to work at the task at hand, or as a lack of seriousness. Work is too important to involve humor. Leaders may present several stories or relate humorous events at the start of a meeting or speech, but the presentations themselves contain little humor.

Most French dislike and avoid the US American practice of beginning a speech with a joke. French speeches almost always begin with a literary or historical allusion. The best start for a business presentation is a quote from a French author that places the general topic within a historical or intellectual framework.

US American humor is seen as crude and unsophisticated. French prefer wit and clever literary references rather than belly laughs. Political jokes and gossip about intellectuals are common forms of French humor. The French do not use humor to release tension; black humor is not a common French type of humor.

Gifts

Gifts are considered to be personal exchanges and are not exchanged by business associates during the first few meetings. Gifts are given only after personal rapport has been established. Gifts packages do not contain the business cards of the donors since doing so suggests the exchanges are formal rather than personal.

The French always appreciate receiving good-quality books. They especially enjoy receiving current bestsellers, histories, biographies, and art books. Like the Germans, French appreciate difficult topics and do not want simplified reading matter. This suggests that they are not intelligent! French of all ages are fascinated by the American West and they enjoy photography books of Western scenes, including American Indians. Most French who visit the United States hope to see the Grand Canyon and redwoods.

A US American guest can always offer adults and children of the family books about the West. The material in children's books is not made as simple in French as it is in the United States and it is best to avoid simple books or those for lower age children. French parents view books for children as more educational than entertaining, and they would not appreciate a book for a child that is too easy and not primarily educational in character. The exceptions are English language books for children learning English. But even these should not be over simplified.

The best gift is hosting a gourmet lunch or dinner. French seldom entertain business associates at home, and they use restaurants as places to entertain. British and US Americans can host lunch in a British-style bar or restaurant. It's best to avoid ethnic restaurants for business entertainment unless the main guest is known to prefer a specific foreign cuisine. The most appreciated meals are in specialized restaurants or in the better-known *haute cuisine* establishments. All better restaurants demand reservations for dinner and reservations are also needed in many restaurants for lunch, especially for large parties.

French businesspersons do not like to receive gifts with company logos and names. They feel such gifts are too commercial. Do not bring wine as a gift when you are invited to dinner. The hosts have decided very carefully which wines should go with the meal. A gift of wine suggests they may not know enough about wines or else it may create havoc with the meal. Wines should not be offered as gifts unless one has returned from a special region; in that case, the wine becomes a novelty. It is best, however, to avoid wine gifts completely.

The French seldom entertain at home. An invitation to someone's home, usually for dinner, is a special occasion. Guests customarily brings flowers (except roses or chrysanthemums) or chocolates. Good quality chocolate is expensive and enjoyed by adults, usually after a meal with coffee and *digestifs*. Many candies are seasonal and care should be given to what candy to offer as a gift. Personnel in specialty *chocolateries* and other candy stores offer expert advice on what is appropriate for which occasion.

✦　　✦　　✦　　✦　　✦

- Flowers should be given in even numbers

- Avoid offering red roses unless you are romantically involved with the receiver

- Carnations are believed to bring bad luck

- Chrysanthemums are associated with death because they are used on graves

✦　　✦　　✦　　✦　　✦

Criticism

The French take criticisms very personally. The French are success-oriented and proud and they avoid failure. Criticisms are seen as personal affronts and good managers avoid making enemies of their subordinates by stating criticisms as indirectly as possible. Direct criticisms are also seen as rude and impolite. Managers avoid direct criticism and excel in diplomacy. Ideally, errors are pointed out as "problems," and French managers intellectualize failures to avoid shaming subordinates. An executive might say, "We have a problem with our shipments." The person who is to blame for the late shipment can then acknowledge that "there is a problem" and that it will be solved immediately without being publicly shamed.

The French have a saying, "*Qui s'excuse, s'accuse* (who excuses himself, accuses himself)." To excuse oneself (to apologize) is to offer a self-accusation, to accept the blame for something. Don't expect apologies from the French, and be prepared not to insist on them.

AN EXERCISE IN *POLITESSE* (POLITENESS)

"Try this exercise in *politesse*: Your neighbor's radio is driving you nuts and you want to do something about it. As an American, I would go the person and say, 'Could you please turn your radio down?' A French person with manners would phrase it differently. 'Have you moved your radio? I never used to hear it before.' The person, if he or she is French, will get the hint."

Harriet Welty Rochefort (1999: 73).

Workers avoid criticizing superiors by either telling them lies or by being silent. French are more tolerant of white lies than are US Americans, in the belief that (1) truth is often relative based on one's perspective; and (2) small lies help avoid blame. A common French attitude is to view lying as diplomacy rather than a major fault. In the same manner, business projections are often exaggerated for better effect and to make the prognosticator look better. Overt liars in France tend to be ignored or indirectly blamed. Giving out unsupported claims that are too positive should be avoided as they will be carefully analyzed and will embarrass the speaker if found to be untrue or unrealistic.

DISTANT ERROR

Adam Gopnick (2000) uses his (French) fax machine to illustrate French attitudes towards errors and mistakes. When there is a problem, the machine displays an error message, the most common of which is *"erreur distante"* or "distant error." The machine displays this message even when the problem is not, in fact, very far away, e.g., when it is out of paper. To the French way of thinking, "the error is distant; the problem lies someplace else; there is always somebody else to blame for your malfunctions" (87).

Subordinates seldom criticize superiors; their responsibilities are to follow orders without volunteering information that might embarrass their superiors.

Bad news that might be taken as criticism of policy is often delivered by a committee of subordinates; this makes potential criticism more impersonal and no single person can be blamed. A committee makes criticism less personal for both sides, especially if a written memorandum is sent before the meeting or is presented during the session.

Criticism also tends to be expressed in writing, in very diplomatic language. Often, criticism is framed in such a way that "the rules" are to blame, not the superior or the one being criticized. This additional strategy also makes the criticism less personal (see also Carroll, 1988).

Language difficulties exist whenever speakers do not use their native languages. Asking someone "Did you understand what I've said" is a normal request but French see this as insulting. They are in essence being criticized for not knowing a language well enough. Assume that misunderstandings will occur if not speaking in French. The correct strategy that does not suggest criticism is to rephrase parts of what has been said. The French are unwilling to admit not having understood something and they will excuse repetition. Another strategy is to ask open-ended questions that do not suggest criticism of language abilities.

In addition, a foreign speaker should never suggest that a French individual has misunderstood what has been said. This is seen as a major type of criticism reserved for children. If in doubt, offer literature that covers the main points of a speech or repeat. You can always suggest that a misunderstanding is your fault; this is the time to be as diplomatic as possible.

Praise

While French superiors avoid direct criticism, they also avoid praising others. In the same manner as Japanese and German managers, French managers expect subordinates to perform according to directions. Doing one's job well is seldom praised because no one should be praised for doing what is expected. In addition, the French are not as goal-oriented as other nationals and achievement is less important than following managerial directives. Since advancement is primarily based on past education and seniority, there is little reason to thank workers for performing well.

In addition, the French in general are pessimistic and feel that few things can be said to be "wonderful" or, especially, "perfect." Saying that a report "is not bad" is praise indeed for the French! By contrast, French dislike the US American propensity to be too optimistic and to praise performance (or anything else) too much. Being too positive seems to the French as bragging, insincerity, or hypocrisy.

Who Should Be Sent To France

The literal meaning of the phrase *savoir faire* is "knowing how to do something." It more commonly denotes a person who is so secure in his knowledge that he remains cool and calm under crisis conditions. The phrase also means being diplomatic and calm under pressure. Having *savoir faire* is a necessary attribute when dealing with French businesspersons. A person who shows impatience or frustration loses respect and is seen as immature.

Dealing with the French also demands persons who are *débrouillard*, meaning talented, resourceful, and self-sufficient, able to use "system D" to achieve their goals.

A sense of style is also a necessary trait. No one will be taken seriously unless he or she is always well dressed in the proper fashion. Even informal activities demand correct clothing that is well pressed and in fashion.

Knowing how to speak French well is expected for those who go to France. French businesspersons do not like to speak a foreign language when in France, though they will do so out of politeness. They feel that foreigners in France should be able to speak French; not doing so is a sign of inferiority.

Being A Businesswoman In France

As in all Latin cultures, women in France are stared at when in public. The correct response to stares is to avoid eye contact. It is still acceptable for a Frenchman to stare openly at passing women. Many make gazing at women a major preoccupation while sitting in a sidewalk café. By contrast, French women in North America and England often feel as if they have become invisible. In those countries, a man offers what Erving Goffman calls "civil inattention." A man looks at a woman (or other man) with a quick glance to acknowledge the other's existence and then is expected to look away to allow for a person's privacy. The US custom is to avoid eye contact, after the initial look, with anyone reaching a distance of eight feet or so. At about eight feet, a person is expected to lower eyes or look elsewhere, in the same manner as an automobile driver dims lights when a car approaches (Goffman, 1993: 84). Men in France are likely to maintain looking at a woman as long as they remain within this area of eight to ten "personal" paces.

The French also have much smaller "personal circles" when using public transportation. Crowded subways and buses result in passengers leaning and pressing against each other as the car sways and passengers push each other back and forth. A woman can complain loudly to the passengers in general if such "accidental" pressing becomes too bothersome (see Carroll, 1988, for further suggestions).

SUGGESTED READINGS

Braganti, Nancy L. and Elizabeth Devine (1992) *European Customs and Manners: How to Make Friends and Do Business in Europe*. New York: Meadowbrook Press.

Moran, Robert T. (1992) *Doing Business in Europe*. Oxford: Heinemann.

Platt, Polly (2000) *Savoir Flair! 211 Tips for Enjoying France and the French*. London: Culture Crossings.

Rochefort, Harriet Welty (2001) *French Fried: The Culinary Capers of an American in Paris*. New York: St. Martin's Press.

Rossman, Marlene L. (1986) *The International Businesswoman: A Guide to Success in the Global Marketplace*. New York: Praeger Special Studies.

Sheppard, Pamela (1994) *Speeches and Presentations in French and English/Discours et exposés en anglais comme en Français*. London: Nicholas Brealey.

Storti, Craig (2001) *Old World/New World: Bridging Cultural Difference: Britain, France, Germany, and the U.S.* Yarmouth, Maine: Intercultural Press.

6
LIVING AND WORKING IN FRANCE

Introduction

Living and working in another country is both easier and harder than simply visiting whether as a tourist or as a businessperson. Being a long-term expatriate becomes easier if one develops a network of friends and acquaintances, so one gains a support system. A support system of friends is there to help out and offer advice when you have questions or when things go wrong, or when you are homesick.

Polly Platt, in her book *French or Foe?* (1995), describes the importance of building up such networks in what she calls her "persistent personal operating" procedure (or PPO). The PPO can also provide the personal touch in cultures in which a personal relationship is necessary to transform a "no can do" into a "can do" situation. Platt describes how the potential headaches of a banal and daily chore such as grocery shopping can be avoided through PPO relations.

In France, customers are expected to offer the correct change if they have it (or at least coins that will enable the clerk simply to return a bill). Merchants in small, neighborhood-based stores often run out of change or seldom have enough for a day's transactions. Clerks also often become irritated (and show it) when customers present them with large bills for small purchases. They will frown and complain to customers if a bill is too large for the transaction. Platt describes how she would shop in the same place every day over a number of years and always chose the same clerk to check her out. She managed to build up a personal relationship with the clerk and eventually would be allowed to "owe" part of the bill when she did not have the correct change. Clerks also are willing to set aside special products for regular customers.

LES MOTS JUSTES

- Expatriate: a person living and working in a foreign country and immersed in its culture

- Sojourner: a person who lives in a foreign country but does not become involved in its culture

- Tourist: a person who visits a foreign country but experiences only the ideal aspects of its culture

Such relationships take time to build up, however, and it is only after living in France for an extended period of time (or as a regular returning visitor) that US Americans generally have the opportunity to make this system work to their advantage.

On the other hand, being in a foreign country for an extended time can present stresses that the short-term tourist and sojourner do not experience. Always thinking and talking in what is not one's native language over a long period of time is frustrating and even self-alienating. Small cultural differences that seem insignificant to the casual visitor can also build up resentment over time; even the simplest interaction presents pitfalls and complications. Expatriates in France can become frustrated over time by unfamiliar foods and ways of behaving. They may feel that nothing is straightforward and that a person can never relax. They instead maintain a constant vigilance that takes its psychological toll over time.

Knowing ahead of time about some of these effects can help reduce this stress as well as increase effectiveness. A partial solution is to plan activities where you can "be yourself" (visits with anglophone friends and family from time to time, preparing foods you're used to, developing support networks, and so on).

Getting Around In France

One great advantage for the US American who lives in France, in contrast to a French individual living in the United States, is that France and Europe in general have extremely well developed networks of efficient and affordable public transportation. It is not really necessary to have a car or use one frequently while working in France. Driving in France is extremely stressful, and finding parking is difficult, expensive, or both. Not using an automobile in French large urban areas such as Paris is in many ways an advantage.

In addition to airlines that offer efficient international and domestic travel, France has an excellent railway system with international, intercity, and local service. The Trans Europe Express (TEE) connects France to other European cities. There is even inter-city service to London via Eurostar—which takes the passenger from the heart of Paris to the center of London in a matter of hours via the "chunnel" (the English channel tunnel)—called "le shuttle" by the French.

The major cities of France are connected by the rapid and comfortable "TGV" (*train à grande vitesse*, or high-speed train). The comfort and speed of the TGV makes it a strong competitor to intra-France airline flights. A TGV ride may cover 250 miles in under two hours. TGV lines link Paris and France's major cities with 3-4 hour trips. Local connections are assured by a combination of the quixotically named slower "*express*" trains and bus services.

The traveler can go almost anywhere in France fairly easily and quickly via public transportation. It may be necessary to change several times and it may take all day, but one can get to even remote areas, though in such cases a private automobile is more practical. Large cities are crisscrossed with networks of trains, subways, and buses. Few places in a French city are more than a short walk from a bus or *métro* (subway) stop.

This said, urban travel involves a lot of walking. Getting to a subway train may involve walking up or down long flights of steps, and changing lines may entail long walks in underground passageways. Both buses and subways may be stiflingly hot in summer, especially when crowded. If you use public transportation in Paris, be prepared for such physical challenges and dress accordingly (wear shoes that are comfortable to walk in, for example). If this is not an option (for example, if you need to look fresh and relaxed upon arrival) either allow plenty of extra time to freshen up, change, relax, etc., in a nearby café before going to your *rendez-vous*, or else consider taking a taxi.

Taxis are always available for local urban travel. Taxis in France seldom cruise for potential fares and remain lined up at taxi stands waiting for customers to come to them. It is also possible to telephone for a taxi to come to one's home or office, but charges begin when the taxi leaves the stand rather than when the customer enters the taxi.

Gasoline and parking are very expensive (gasoline is roughly US$5 a gallon) so that many French persons prefer not to own a car and rely instead on public transportation. Even car owners tend to use public transportation most of the time. Cars in France come out to clog highways during evenings, on weekends, and during the summer vacation months.

Paris, like other large French cities, has many commuters who arrive each morning from the suburbs in rush hour crowds. The rhyming slang saying for the commuter cycle is *métro-boulot-dodo* (subway-work-sleep) and reflects the French view of the disliked repetitive work. Many French individuals commute several hours each way to work in order to remain in a large city or in one's natal town while working in a large city. Many "*turbo profs*" live in Paris, the cultural and intellectual center of France, but work as faculty at universities throughout the country. They teach a few days each week at their workplace and return to Paris for the rest of the week.

France's three largest cities, Paris, Lyon, and Marseilles, all have subway systems. There are also excellent inter-and intra-urban bus and train systems. Paris visitors can easily learn how to travel throughout the city. The *Plan-Guide Répertoire des Rues de Paris*, in its distinctive red cover, provides instant directions to any part of Paris and the suburbs. The guide contains an index to streets and their nearest *métro* stations, street maps, addresses of museums, embassies, churches, hospitals, movie theaters and other important destinations, as well as subway and bus routes. A few minutes' study of the *Plan-Guide* allows a visitor to travel easily to all Paris sites.

There are sixteen *métro* lines in Paris and most addresses are within 500 yards of a *métro* station. *Métro* service begins at 5:30 a.m. and continues until the last train or bus reaches its station at 1:00 a.m. Tickets can be purchased individually, but are cheaper when purchased as a *carnet* (booklet) of ten tickets. The fare is a flat rate regardless of how many connections ("*correspondances*") one makes, provided one remains within a single zone (central Paris is all within zone 1). Longer journeys may require more tickets (the zones are marked on subway maps). Those staying in Paris for several days can buy unlimited passes for three and five days. Riders keep their stamped tickets until they have exited the subway system because ticket inspectors can impose fines on those who do not have validly stamped tickets ("*un titre de transport*"), and sometimes the ticket is needed to exit.

Those staying in Paris longer may be entitled to use a weekly pass ("*carte hebdomadaire*," also known as the "*carte orange*"), or even an annual one. In this case, you will need to fill out a form that you can obtain from the *métro* offices. You will need to have passport-size pictures of yourself (the kind you purchase at a booth in the mall usually work fine). The weekly card is valid from Monday to Sunday and can be purchased ahead of time at local *bureaux de tabac* (as well as in the *métro*). As of 2002, the weekly card costs 13.25 euros (for zone 1; you can choose a more expensive card that covers more zones if your commute requires it), or roughly the equivalent of $13. Make certain that the first time you use the card, it gets stamped ("*composté*"). In the *métro*, this happens automatically when you put the ticket in the gate to enter, but on the buses, you must stamp the ticket yourself. (You must also stamp train tickets) This is to prevent people from using the same ticket for another journey that they have not paid for.

Waiting In Line

The French do not like to wait patiently in line, such as for a bus or subway car. Except for queues in government offices and post offices, lines in France are "me first" affairs. French people are too individualistic to wait patiently in lines for their turn. Lines to board buses involve pushing and a certain amount of shoving. The normal rules of courtesy among French are ignored in lines. Anglo-Saxons not used to this behavior need to learn to be more aggressive than in their country of origin. The French consider this merely assertiveness, rather than aggression.

Being A Guest

The philosopher Simone de Beauvoir did much of her writing in cafés, illustrating the large extent public spaces such as cafés and restaurants are used for personal purposes. She also seldom entertained in her home and only very close friends were allowed in her hotel room or, later in life, in her apartment. Being invited to someone's house initiates a new stage of friendship or intimacy and is rare among business associates.

Elevators in older buildings tend to be small. "Up" people have priority and the custom is for guests to ride up and walk down.

✦ ✦ ✦ ✦ ✦

LES MOTS JUSTES

The French use the expression *"renvoyer l'ascenseur"* (to send the elevator back) in common parlance to convey the idea of returning courtesies or favors. In many buildings, the small elevator doesn't automatically return to the ground floor and a person arriving in the building must first send for the elevator and wait for it to descend before being able to use it. A thoughtful person will, after using the elevator, press the button for the ground floor (the *"rez de chaussée"* or RC) so that the elevator is there waiting for the next person to enter the building. Of course, one is more likely to do this if one knows there is someone waiting to use it and one wishes to be courteous, hence the expression.

✦ ✦ ✦ ✦ ✦

Strikes

Strikes and work blockages are very common in France. To the French, a strike is a form of civil demonstration or political protest. Strikers often take to the street to voice their complaints. Another distinct feature of strikes and demonstrations in France is the frequency with which government workers strike for better pay and increased job security. Politicians have very little power over civil servants, and it is impossible for government officials to stop civil servants from striking or to punish them for doing so.

The government bureaucracy is the real power in France, and bureaucrats can usually ignore elected officials when they wish to do so. Consequently, one of the most effective forms of protest is strikes and activities that incapacitate the public sector and embarrass politicians, who are blamed for the inconvenience of strikes by the public. During the spring of 2000, tax collectors in France, of which there are

136,000, locked their offices and demonstrated in the streets. Their grievance was that government officials' attempts to reform the tax office would threaten tax collectors' job security. One proposal that threatened jobs was to simplify tax procedures so that taxpayers would have to deal with only one office instead of the current average of five distinct offices. As a result, the collection of taxes in France costs three times as much per taxpayer than it does in the United States.

Farmers who wish to demand higher crop subsidies block roads with truckloads of potatoes, tomatoes, or apples. Farmers have also blocked roads leading into Italy and Spain to protest the importation of cheaper wine from those countries. These protests almost always take place during May through September.

LES MOTS JUSTES

A strike in French is *"une grève."* The word means a riverbank and its use to refer to labor actions comes from the spot on the bank of the Seine in front of the *Hôtel de Ville* (City Hall) in Paris where workers would gather to present their grievances to the authorities. Many strikes in France are demonstrations to force politicians to take certain political actions rather than to demand higher pay.

In 1998, for example, Air France stewards and stewardesses went on strike just two weeks before soccer's World Cup final competitions were to be held in France. During August, 1999, farmers protesting possible US tariffs increases on the importation of French foie gras, cheeses, mustard, and truffles dumped tons of manure, vegetables, and fruit in front of a number of branches of McDonald's. Foreigners traveling in France during the spring and summer months have to be

patient and be prepared for strikes that disrupt transportation, communication, or production.

Strikes by museum personnel have recently closed major Parisian
museums. Another recent strike which also inconvenienced tourists
was by the transportation workers of Paris in response to the fatal
assault of a ticket controller; union workers were demanding more protection for *métro* personnel. In 2002, it was the turn of air traffic con-
trollers to go on strike.

- During strikes and road blockages, only the most necessary services continue: ambulances, police, and bakeries

- Transport workers tend to strike during the summer months
  and production decreases because many workers cannot travel
  to work

- Many schedules during the summer cannot be met due to delays
  from strikes. Be patient when delays occur

Given the general reliance on public transportation in France, it
comes as no surprise that the country is quickly paralyzed by any strike
that affects the transportation system, whether it be airlines or the Paris
subway (and their sympathetic comrades in transport unions in other
cities).

The French themselves phlegmatically accept strikes as a regular and
normal part of life and often refer, half-jokingly, to the "strike season."
Most strikes are in the spring and summer, when the tourist and vacation seasons are in full swing (for maximum efficiency). Strikes in the
middle of winter are rare, but almost every summer visitor to France
can count on experiencing at least one strike. The French pride them-

selves on being able to maintain their daily schedules, though transportation-related strikes cause high absenteeism among workers.

Foreign visitors, especially US Americans, are puzzled by the French's acceptance of strikes as a "natural" phenomenon. Foreigners used to strikes being limited to factories or stores do not understand why strikes in France are so public and why they are aimed at inconveniencing the public as much as possible.

The French are not oblivious to the inconvenience of strikes, since commuters during these periods often face four-hour (or longer) traffic jams to drive to work in Paris and everyone's temper is frayed. But at the same time, there is something of a carnival-like atmosphere where public formality is relaxed. Normally aloof passengers bond on the sidewalk or in subway stations as they exchange the latest news and information about which buses or trains may be running and when a transportation strike might be over. The French during these strikes tend also to be philosophical and accept, though not necessarily gracefully, the fact that work and daily life will be disrupted.

The French are likely to accept the fact that meetings cannot take place during strikes and that all schedules are delayed a few hours or cancelled completely. Many workers may arrive several or more hours late for work and soon will leave to start the long journey of a few hours home, but feel they have done their duty by showing up for work (even if nothing gets done). Foreigners should also develop a more fatalistic attitude toward work delays and inefficiencies when strikes occur.

This fatalistic acceptance of strikes by the French public derives in part from a general sense of sympathy for the principle of trades unions and a feeling of solidarity towards those who are in conflict with authority. While not everyone in France feels this way, for many persons their acceptance of strikes is an extension of the widespread French assumption that jobs must be made to fit people and not people their jobs. That is, workers do not exist primarily to service customers. It is secondary that customers might be inconvenienced by a strike.

People who work come first rather than customers or the general public. Strikes are tolerated among the French because they may be necessary to accomplish better work conditions. There may be grumbling about the traffic conditions, food shortages, or other inconveniences, but this attitude is less often aimed at the striking workers in France than others. There is a tendency to blame the government for allowing the causes of a strike to exist.

Making Friends

Making friends in France is difficult because French are cautious about developing friendships with strangers and they seldom warm to those without an introduction or reference of some type. Nor do the French easily develop friendships with neighbors. Residential proximity is not seen as a good reason for friendship. There is too much sense of residential privacy to invite strangers into one's house. Generally, French individuals entertain at home only close friends and relatives.

Friendships can be made based on common interests and references. Making one French friend leads easily to more friendships. However, the process of making friends is very slow compared with that experienced by US Americans.

Shopping In France

Stores are generally open from nine a.m. to five p.m. (later in Paris). Many close from noon to two o'clock. Most smaller stores are closed on Sundays and Mondays, including groceries and even department stores. Larger retail establishments such as the "hypermarket" Carrefour are open throughout the day. Many neighborhood grocery stores remain open until late into the evening, however.

Shopping in France remains largely a local affair. The French economy supports a "mom and pop" system of distribution consisting of family-owned and operated retail establishments. Each neighborhood in France's large cities contains its own selection of stores. Most French shop for groceries several days a week to ensure that produce and other foods are fresh. Higher cost at small neighborhood stores is the price French shoppers are willing to pay for convenience, personal attention, and freshness.

Many neighborhoods have their own distinct character. A sign of sophistication among the French is knowing where the best items can be located throughout a city. Just as someone living in New York or Chicago may seek out the best place to get pizza or bagels, the French shopper has his or her favorite places to find special items such as chocolates, wine, or cheeses. Someone wishing for honey and almond pastries might go to the Moslem quarter to shop at an Algerian bakery.

There are also many large retail outlets, such as the large department stores and *hypermarchés* (super-supermarkets that are twice or more the size of Wal-Marts in the United States). The latter are located outside of cities on highway loops meant to be frequented by automobile users. A visit to an *hypermarché* offers insights on French buying habits and consumer tastes.

Many department stores in Paris and elsewhere were established during the nineteenth century, and their buildings are considered national treasures of interior design and architecture and these are listed in all tourist guidebooks. Some have modernized to some extent, but most remain traditional in product presentation. *Au Bon Marché*, the *Galeries Lafayette*, and *La Samaritaine* are some of the most famous *grands magasins* (large department stores) in Paris.

Other department stores, such as *Au Printemps* have attempted to modernize, though they have maintained their original buildings. *Au Printemps*, for example, has rollerblading salespersons equipped with wireless video cameras. Potential customers can ask to see selected products on one of the store's websites. The clerk types the caller's size and color and style preferences as she skates to the product requested. Clerks will even stand in front the the video camera and hold up items. *Au Printemps'* main store in Paris has twenty floors and 50,000 squares of space for its 1.5 million items (Delaney, 1999).

Fresh bread is considered both an essential food item and a craft. Bakers are proud of their skills and many have their own specialties. Many older shoppers still shop daily or twice a day for fresh bread since French bread contains no preservatives and goes stale quickly. Bread not eaten in the morning or at noon is often grilled or toasted as part of a light family supper. Yesterday's bread is also a staple of morning breakfast in typical families. Except for breakfast, bread is eaten without butter or jams. While it is not necessary to eat large portions of bread, a meal is considered incomplete without a serving of bread. The government subsidizes bread production and bread is, unlike most other foods in France, relatively inexpensive. Baking is a respected profession and the French government offers annual prizes for winners of national competitions in baking. As one would expect, there are many different types of loaves available fresh daily.

Boulangerie: Pocket Guide to Paris's Famous Bakeries by Jack Armstrong and Dolores Wilson (Berkeley: Ten Speed Press, 1999) describes the best bakeries in Paris by *arrondissement* (neighborhood). Other cities such as Lyon, Bordeaux and Marseilles as well as regions (Alsace, Normandy, etc.) all have their own shopping and eating guides for breads, wines, beers, restaurants, etc.

It may come as a surprise to the American businessperson or expatriate how much regulation there is in France dealing with retail issues. Even sales ("*soldes*"), when goods are sold at reduced prices, are controlled down to the level of when sales can begin and how long they are allowed to last. While many of these restrictions are decades old, some have been enacted as late as 1996. An item sold "on sale" must show both the regular and the sale price. The regular price must be the price charged by the store during the last thirty days preceding the sale (not, for example, the highest price ever charged by the store or the manufacturers' suggested price). A store cannot bring in merchandise just for the sale, and when the sales goods are sold, no rain checks are allowed. The restocking of a sales item during the sale period is defined by the French government as a special offer (*une promotion*) rather than part of a sale (*une solde*). Officials conduct spot checks to ensure that the rules on sales and promotions are being followed.

A note of caution to shoppers. Smaller, neighborhood stores seldom provide shopping bags for their customers, so be prepared. French shoppers usually carry a net bag to stow their purchases. Since the French prefer shopping several times a week, most purchases are few enough to be placed in one bag.

Eating And Drinking

The act of eating is both social and intellectual. Interesting conversation and good food go together and are a vital part of good living. The French take eating very seriously and see it as a major social occasion. One survey indicated that the French devote an average of almost two hours to their main meal (versus 1.2 hours in the United States). They may not eat much more (and probably eat less) than US Americans, but food and good conversation are savored and enjoyed slowly and with ceremony. A dramatic example of the seriousness about food is the suicide of the Prince of Condé's (1621-86) chef because the seafood had not arrived for a banquet in honor of the French king.

Eating together is often the first indication that a closer relationship is being developed. A casual invitation for a drink (*"on prend un verre?"*) at a café or bistro is a mark of a beginning friendship. Virtually every small village and neighborhood has numerous cafés where people can congregate and socialize. Since bars and cafés allow customers to stay as long as they wish, one does not have to drink much; the main purposes of sitting at a table in a sidewalk café are more to socialize, see others, and be seen.

Although cafés and bars are informal establishments, customers are expected to follow traditional etiquette. Customers should be quiet and not disturb others (though crowding is common). Waiters are addressed with the formal *vous* forms and a *bonjour* and *au revoir* are made upon arriving and leaving. Tips in addition to those included as the service charge in the bills are customary if the service has been warmer and more attentive than usual. Remember, however, that many waiters (and sales clerks) do not include smiling as one of their duties. They are there to provide a service, not to be friends. In most cafés, once you have purchased a drink, you may continue to sit undisturbed for as long as you like.

Cafés must display their prices (the "*tarif des consommations*") but cafés and bars have two price lists based on whether a customer sits at a table or stands at the bar ("*au comptoir*"). A soft drink and lunch may cost up to twice as much according to whether one sits or stands. It is not acceptable to purchase a beverage at the counter, then carry it over to a table and sit down.

Cafés are required to maintain restrooms available to the public, sometimes for a small fee. It is customary to order something before using the facilities.

The two-hour business lunch is still common, though less so now than in the past. A six- or seven-course meal may take as much as three hours. Family gatherings usually include a major meal that can last four to six or more hours, though there are rests between courses.

✦　✦　✦　✦　✦

TYPES OF EATING ESTABLISHMENTS

- *Restaurant*: serious place to eat
- *Café*: serves beverages and light meals such as sandwiches

- *Brasserie*: Large beer pub often serving German foods

- *Bistro*: neighborhood bar serving food. The French version of "fast food"

- *Auberge*: country inn serving local specialties

- *Tabac*: bar serving coffee and alcoholic drinks; includes a counter where one buys telephone cards, *métro* tickets, cigarettes, etc.

All restaurants except the most expensive are expected to have low cost set meals ("*repas touristiques*"). All restaurants list these bargains, sometimes called simply "*le menu*" (as opposed to "*la carte*," which lists all the food served), along with other offerings on a display near the front door. Potential diners in France wander and look at menus until they see selections and prices they accept. There are also fixed-priced menus that list exactly which courses are included in a meal for different prices (smaller restaurants may allow substitution). Otherwise the diner orders *à la carte* and selects the items desired and pays accordingly. Most restaurants offer a *menu dégustation* (tasting menu) containing a variety of the chef's specialties in small portions.

In Paris, restaurants are open from noon to two or a little later and from 7:30 to 10:30 in the evening. Smaller eateries such bars are more flexible when they are open and cafés are usually open from early in the morning until late at night. One can usually get sandwiches and omelets in bars almost at any time. Some brasseries are open 24 hours. All food bills ("*l'addition*") include a fifteen percent tip and a 18.6% tax. In restaurants, the bill is seldom brought to the table until requested. Café and bar clientele may stay at their tables after a bill has been presented until they wish to leave. Customers stay as long as they wish, within reason (longer at cafés than at restaurants). In French eating establishments of all types, it would be considered rude to hurry customers away, especially if the reason for doing so was just to make more money by turning over tables faster. In American restaurants it is considered good service to clear away eating dishes as soon as the customer has finished (it is not only French visitors to the USA who feel irritated by over-zealous servers who try to whip away plates before the last mouthful has disappeared). In France, on the other hand, it would be considered insulting to clear away the dishes from the last course before the customer leaves (it might imply that you are trying to hurry them away). Lingering over the meal is part of its pleasure, and leaving plates on the table is not a sign of inattention on the part of the staff.

The correct place for hands (whether or not they are holding a knife and fork) is with wrists resting lightly on the table. Old established rules of etiquette require that hands are never placed on the lap during a meal and must remain visible at all times. Otherwise, French table manners are similar to the US American version except the former are more formal. Both countries reject similar eating behaviors, though there are some specific differences:

- Don't eat with your mouth open
- Don't order foods that are messy to eat in a business context
- Don't touch your food with hands except for bread
- Don't eat too much
- Eat everything that is offered
- Eat everything that is placed on your plate
- Don't place elbows on the table or slouch
- Wipe your mouth with a napkin before drinking
- The fork is held in the left hand and the knife in the right

- Lettuce is served in large pieces, folded by the fork and never cut
- Don't bite off pieces of bread

A few more comments are in order about appreciating good food and drink in France. French children are raised to eat everything that is put in front of them and to clean their plates. They grow up to like everything considered edible, which is a wider range than for most US Americans. French distinguish between good and bad tasting versions of the same food, a distinction almost unknown to average Americans.

US Americans value freedom and independence of choice: a person has the right to choose to eat or refuse certain things. A person has the freedom to express her own personality by choosing what she eats. To the French, personal expressions of choice seem childish and overly fastidious; one should learn to eat whatever is considered edible and avoid low quality rather than categories of foods. The concept of "health foods," for example, barely exists in France, though the French are buying more "*biologique*" (organic) produce. Some stores accept orders for produce that are picked and delivered the same day to guarantee freshness. The French way of thinking is that ingredients are unhealthy when they are artificially produced (hence the resistance to growth hormones in beef or to genetically modified organisms ("*OGMs*" in French) or eaten in too large a quantity.

There is therefore no need for a separate category of "health foods." One doesn't need skimmed milk, "*lait écrémé*" (though it is available in France) but one simply drinks less whole milk, because whole milk is "more natural" and tastes better. Instead of eating fat-free sour cream, eat fewer dishes that call for cream sauces.

Most French consider vegetarianism to be an aberration, though vegetarian restaurants exist in Paris. Special food requests in general are seen more as bizarre and it is better to be traditional in one's taste. One can usually order omelets or salads to avoid food allergies and to accommodate vegetarianism, except at gourmet restaurants.

The US American attitude that the customer is king holds less sway in French restaurants and in matters of food, the best chefs know better than the consumers what is proper to eat and how to prepare food (don't ask for condiments such as ketchup or steak sauce), or else why go to a good restaurant? Chefs and waiters will not hesitate to tell you what is good that day or what you should order. Of course, it is appropriate to complain when the ingredients or preparation are below standard. But the statement "I do not like this" has little meaning to the French.

Similarly, food allergies (for example to wheat) are virtually unknown in France. Observance of religious food preparation rituals (e.g., Jewish kosher laws) are seen by the French as theoretically legitimate but viewed as nuisances. French Catholics shop at kosher butcher shops because they feel the meats there are fresher and better tasting. The rationales are quality and taste rather than religious.

The US American current fashion for white wine means that one occasionally hears American tourists in French restaurants saying, "I only drink white wine." The French see this attitude as the height of affectation and ignorance because the appropriate wine is determined by what is served and not by individual choice. Rejecting a wine based on its color seems as arbitrary to the French as someone saying, "I don't eat any vegetables that are round or yellow." US Americans who don't like red wine shouldn't order red meat dishes or meat dishes with heavy sauces though the rule red-with-red-meat-only is not absolute, but influenced by sauce and preparation.

About ten percent of the French population abstains from drinking any alcohol. Unfortunately, many dishes are made with small amounts of alcohol and this is not always evident from menus. Cooks often don't think of alcohol as alcohol when used in cooking, but more like a spice. The alcohol is cooked away in recipes calling for alcohol and the dishes retain only the taste of the beverage, as in *poulet au whiskey*.

There are alternatives to drinking wine with meals, including a wide range of brand-name mineral waters (no one in France drinks milk except babies). Tap water is now safe to drink throughout France and a diner can always ask for tap water rather than paying extra for bottled water by asking for "*une carafe d'eau*" (never ask just for "*de l'eau*"). A medical excuse is always acceptable as a good reason to abstain from alcohol. If some alcohol is tolerable, accept one glass of recommended wine and sip a small portion during the meal. Leaving a glass nearly full is a signal that you have had enough and do not want a refill. An empty glass will almost automatically be re-filled.

Wine and alcohol are considered as a food or as something that enhances food. It is seldom drunk without food. Public drunkenness is frowned upon and no one should drink wine too much or too fast. Alcohol is considered an adult taste, but not a taboo, and wine is served regularly to staff and teachers at school cafeteria lunches, for example.

Regional wines have maintained their popularity and French individuals are expected to be familiar with local wine varieties as well as the major vintages. Restaurant managers take pride in their wine cellars and are happy to recommend the house specialties. All restaurants aspiring to gourmet status offer *vins maison* or house specialty wines. These are usually of excellent quality and relatively inexpensive.

In spite of France's well-deserved reputation for fine wines (*vin d'appellation contrôlée* means something like a "brand name"), most French drink ordinary, cheaper wines called *vins de table* (table wines) during normal occasions such as family meals. These ordinary, non-vintage wines are the equivalent to mid-priced, or less, California wines. (Few French would admit that many California wines are as good as many French wines.) Cheaper *vins ordinaires* are often a mix of rougher Algerian and Italian wines with smoother French wines. Ordinary wines do not label the origin of their wines and many contain foreign wines. Residents often bring their own bottles to their neighborhood wine dealer to fill up on these cheaper wines. Working class Frenchmen often drink a glass or two of these cheaper wine mixtures with water during work breaks.

It is best not to praise Italian wines to the French. Italy produces and exports more wine than does France, and its table wines are as good or better than their French equivalents. French winegrowers periodically block highways on the French-Italian border and overturn large container trucks carrying cheaper Italian wines into France.

No matter what, a diner should treat food seriously, praise it when warranted, and praise the choice and preparation. The worst crime in France is to be indifferent to food (to eat merely to live) and to say, "I don't care what or where we eat as long as it's quick." The French are proud of the fact that they "live to eat" while other nationalities, they believe, don't appreciate food and are examples of the "eat to live" attitude. The latter is an insult to the French. It is no accident that Disney officials state that Euro-Disney offers better food than the other Disney theme parks in the USA and Japan.

The French have not yet accepted the concept of "food courts" as too lacking in seriousness and as a discouragement of food quality. Food courts are seen as too "mechanical." Food courts also are disliked by the French because French diners are less loyal to brand names. National restaurant food chains are relatively unknown in France. The exception is when a famous chef opens a second restaurant. There are seldom multiple restaurants on a national level sponsored by a chef.

There is a correlation between social class and size of food portions. Generally, the lower classes serve more substantial foods and larger servings, traditionally consistent with great manual labor demands. The higher classes exchange quantity for quality, and portions are usually arranged before food is served at the table. Someone who eats too much is a *gourmand* rather than a respected *gourmet* and is considered uncouth and lower class. The French do not snack between meals as much as US Americans to better enjoy their meals (to stay thin).

More informal family meals and those prepared for members of the middle and lower classes tend to involve larger serving dishes placed on the dining table. Taking seconds from such dishes is acceptable, though it is better to wait until the hostess offers additional portions unless the diner is a close friend.

Bread is usually served pre-cut in a basket. When you take a piece, it is always placed on the table, not on one's plate, usually to one's left (at the "ten o'clock" in relation to the dinner plate). Don't worry about making crumbs! That's what the tablecloth is for. Do not bite off your bread, but break off bite-size pieces with your fingers.

Eating too much is seen as lower class (*déclassé*) behavior and is inappropriate for businesspersons. One should focus on conversation and food appreciation during meals rather than appearing to be famished by eating and drinking large amounts.

Do not expect much choice beyond the established menu when going to a French restaurant. Attempts to order inappropriate or special demands will elicit pity, scorn, outrage, resistance, and even insults.

A major difference in eating practices between France and English-speaking countries is that, in France, the chef rules. Restaurant goers in France seldom add condiments such as salt and pepper and bottled sauces (e.g., ketchup, mustard, etc.) to their food. Adding even salt at the table may be seen as a gesture that the food was not properly prepared. Such actions may anger the cook, and waiters may refuse to bring extra condiments to your table. It is best to accept restaurant food as offered. French cooks are as proud of their sauces and selection of spices as they are of their foods. On the other hand, French diners can be very vocal if a meal is not well prepared and if the materials are not fresh or appropriate.

The senior author once selected to eat at a small restaurant in Paris one summer. This restaurant contained roughly twenty tables (all but one other empty). The author ordered a wine from the Cahors region to complement his meat dish; Cahors wines are among his favorites though they are not *grands crus*. The chef-waiter stiffened when he heard the wine selection. He suggested that Cahors wines, though available, were too heavy to be drunk during the summer. After vainly pleading that the customer really wanted a Cahors, the customer asked for his recommendation. The waiter brightened and even smiled. He suggested several other appropriate wines, became friendlier, and made other suggestions concerning the meal.

Business meals tend to be formal affairs, especially when they take place in the evenings. A mark of courtesy is the offering of toasts. The host is expected to offer a toast in greeting at the beginning of the meal, or soon after. The honored guest is not expected to join in the toast and drink with the others. This guest is expected to offer a toast in turn later during the meal. The best time to offer a returning toast is just before or after the introduction of a course. Toasts are short and to the point. They usually deal with expressions of gratitude for the meal, entertainment, and welcome. Toast themes can also express pleasure at doing business with the host and company, expressions of French culture and cultural sites visited, and expressions of friendship. The latter should not be too effusive or they will seem to be insincere.

Being pleasant to the public is a matter of individual decision. The French sense of individualism encourages French waiters to believe that they are paid to serve as professionally as possible; they have not sold their personalities. French waiters never introduce themselves by name. In spite of the stereotype from movies, a customer should call a French waiter "*monsieur*" rather than "*garçon*." *Mademoiselle* is acceptable for waitresses. A simple "*s'il vous plaît*" is often enough to get the staff's attention. Never click your fingers to get attention. You'll get it, but not the kind you want.

Customers need to be pleasant first in order to receive more personal service and attention from waiters and clerks. That is why it is important to use proper titles and establish a personal rapport with those who serve customers. A waiter or clerk who likes a customer becomes more cooperative, gives admirable advice, and may be (slightly) more attentive.

While tipping practices in France are similar to those in the United States, there remain a few differences. Being a waiter is considered a career and a profession. Tips are included in a meal's bill and are part of a waiter's salary. Additional tipping for unusually good service is rare, and extra tips are generally smaller than in the United States. On smaller bills, simply rounding up is sufficient and the waiter keeps the coins. All menus and bills will include the words *service compris* if the tip, or service, is included in the price of the dishes. In the event that the bill states "*service non compris*," this means that the tip has not been included. In this case, it is customary to leave a tip of fifteen or so percent.

Family dinners in French homes tend to be formal affairs whenever there are guests. Most French eat dinner fairly late, and meals may start at eight or nine p.m. Because of this, it is acceptable to telephone persons until almost midnight; a formal dinner that starts at nine will almost certainly not be finished until eleven or later. People tend not to go to bed until near midnight.

Smoking And Other Hazards

Unlike certain areas where France is more regulated than the United States, France has much less regulation when it comes to smoking. US Americans are often scandalized that restaurants do not provide non-smoking areas and that they are almost never greeted by the now-common phrase "smoking or non-smoking?" ("*fumeur*" or "*non-fumeur*") In certain spaces, such as trains, there is non-smoking seating, but the policy is routinely violated and seldom enforced. Fellow passengers can ask the smoker not to smoke in the train's seating area, and most smokers will go and smoke in the aisle or at the end of the coaches. There is, however, little concern among the French with the effects of second-hand smoke.

Smoking is prohibited when doing so might create a fire hazard, such as in libraries or work areas. In most offices and most public places where people gather for social and personal reasons, such as cafés, bars, and restaurants, smoking is widely accepted and the right to smoke is strongly defended as a form of individual freedom. Protest is seen in these places as another example of US American hypocrisy and Puritanism. These attitudes are slowly changing, as the French government exposes the public to anti-smoking information, but by and large, smoking is seen as an individual decision, not something that justifies public policing.

Expatriates visiting or living in France should be prepared to deal with the smoking issue. If bothered by smoke, one strategy is to choose outdoor seating whenever possible. If it is necessary to ask others not to smoke, consider effective ways of doing so other than a lecture on public health.

Another health hazard (in American eyes especially) to which the French seem amazingly impervious is the issue of ubiquitous dog waste on the sidewalks, something few visitors to Paris or other large French urban areas have avoided noticing. The problem can cause frustration and embarrassment, but also has more serious consequences as when it causes pedestrians to slip and fall, sometimes causing serious injury.

✦   ✦   ✦   ✦   ✦

LES MOTS JUSTES

Moto-crottes: (f.) A motorbike with a suction tube used by Parisian municipal authorities to try to cope with the dogwaste problem on sidewalks. For more information on linguistic insights into French culture, see Levieux and Levieux (1999). The "*motto-crottes*" is one of many words listed in this useful dictionary. Words are listed alphabetically in French with brief definitions in English, examples of French usage, and occasional cultural notes. The work is a valuable resource for those living or working in France who encounter new words in French. Many words are drawn from business, commerce, and politics.

Parisians themselves are not blind to this blot on the French reputation caused by dog messes in public places. Solving this problem, however, has proved a challenge. An owner whose dog fouls the sidewalk can be fined, but this penalty is seldom invoked and seems to have had little deterrent effect. In the fall of 1999, authorities in Paris tried a humorous poster and movie-short campaign to try to encourage dog walkers to take more responsibility, but with no noticeable consequences. Grates around some sidewalk trees have been designated (by signs with outlines of dogs) as appropriate places for canine defecation, but French dogs, like their owners, insist on their individuality and freedom.

Visitors must copy the indigenous French solution: watch where you walk! This is hard for many tourists wanting to see the sights, but it doesn't mean walking around with downcast eyes all of the time. It merely means being more alert and glancing down frequently to see what lies ahead, part of the "streetwise" repertoire of skills of many city dwellers around the world.

For those who want to venture further into the French psyche, understanding (as opposed simply to learning to cope with) the apparent indifference to dog waste can be a useful exercise. To the French, dog waste is a fact of life and therefore something natural, albeit somewhat distasteful. It must be avoided, but not necessarily hidden. This goes along with some of the French food practices that shock Americans. While French open-air markets can be quaint and picturesque, US Americans can be shocked to see freshly killed meat for sale, skinned whole rabbits or unplucked chickens all hanging in the open, non-refrigerated markets. Live animals are also sold to be butchered at home to guarantee freshness. To the French, Americans are hypocritical about where meat comes from, buying miscellaneous parts that are no longer identifiable as coming from an animal. They also feel that Americans are unreasonable to reject horsemeat, which the French believe is tastier and healthier than beef. Many traditional recipes for sick persons include broths made from horsemeat.

Hotel Living

Most foreigners staying in France for business reasons will find themselves staying at a hotel. Many hotels cater to long-term guests by offering weekly rates or discounts for longer stays. Not long ago it was not uncommon for people to live permanently in hotels. The existentialist philosopher Simone de Beauvoir, for example, spent a good part of her professional life living in various hotels, and she did not move to an apartment until late in life (Bair, 1990).

Many hotels in France are still privately owned and operated by a family. Only larger hotels are part of a chain, and many of these are still privately owned and local in nature. The French hotel industry, similar to its retail establishments, has not experienced the consolidation found in the United States. There are both advantages and disadvantages to this French localism of the hotel industry. On the one hand, hotels are frequently smaller and less impersonal than in the United States. It is possible to receive much personal attention if one is a frequent guest.

On the other hand, it is sometimes harder to know what to expect from the staff of these smaller hotels as they are somewhat different from one another. Some generalizations are possible, however. These slight differences often add charm to a stay.

In most hotels, a continental breakfast is included in the price of the room ("*le petit déjeuner est compris*") unless the hotel caters primarily to foreign tourists. Smaller hotels may not posses full restaurant facilities and breakfast may be limited to pastries and hot beverages. Special items such as fruit juice or eggs may not be available or are charged a premium. There may also be a surcharge for having breakfast delivered to one's room, though the public eating area near the lobby tends to be cozy and friendly. Smaller hotels, as well as large, deluxe establishments, usually forbid cooking in rooms and do not provide space for cooking (or much else). Hotel personnel also take a very dim view of a guest's inquiries concerning delivery of take-out food. On the other hand, smaller hotels are always located near excellent small restaurants offering relatively low cost meals.

It is also assumed that guests in smaller hotels will treat hotel property with respect, not have parties in their rooms, and will not hang laundry out of the window or any other place in the room. Nor will the staff allow loud noises and boisterous behavior that disturb other guests. Many of these hotels shut down fairly early in the evening. The bar might be closed after ten o'clock or so, and it may be difficult to send out faxes after the day staff has gone off-duty.

Especially in the smaller, more economical hotels, bathroom facilities may or may not be part of the room. Inquire first to get details if the room includes a shower stall and toilet. All will have sinks. Hotels ranked with two stars or less seldom have complete bathroom facilities. The guest may have to schedule the use of a bath located down the hall.

Smaller hotels (and larger ones) charge high fees for the use of a telephone. Frequent hotel guests in France receive incoming calls in their hotel rooms but go out to use a public telephone for outgoing calls.

One very important generalization is that, as in every area of dealing with the French, it pays to take a few moments to establish personal relationships with the owner, manager, and staff of one's hotel. Greeting the manager and desk staff each day with a *"Bonjour monsieur/ madame"* and exchanging pleasantries about the weather, etc. is all that is required for receiving more personal attention. You will find that your mail and faxes are passed along to you promptly and that any obstacles or difficulties you run into will be that much easier to solve. A manager will also make calls in French for you if a personal relationship has begun.

In French hotels, it is expected that guests will drop off their keys at the front desk each time they go out and pick them up again on returning (in contrast to the US American hotel practice where guests come and go without ever returning to the front desk once they have checked in). In France, this key ritual is an excellent way to establish a personal relationship with hotel staff, if only to find out if you have messages. If you do not stop at the front desk (to drop off or pick up your key), the staff may not feel they have a responsibility to seek you out to tell you that you have a message.

The hotel manager can also offer recommendations on where to eat, where to get dry cleaning done, find the nearest pharmacy, how to buy tickets for entertainment, etc. Desk personnel will also be more willing to call for a taxi, lend a hand with luggage and provide minor services that are not automatically made in smaller hotels.

SUGGESTED READINGS

Gendlin, Frances (1998) *Culture Shock! Paris at Your Door*. Portland, Oregon: Graphic Arts Publishing Company.

Hawkinson, Anni and Patrick R. Moran (1994) *Living in France*. Bratleboro, Vermont: Pro Lingua Associates.

Miller, Stuart (1990) *Understanding Europeans*. Santa Fe, New Mexico: John Muir.

Newman, Eva (1997) *Going Abroad: The Bathroom Survival Guide*. Saint Paul, Minnesota: Marlor Press, Inc.

Stein, Gail (1999) *The Complete Idiot's Guide to Learning French* (second edition). Indianapolis: Macmillan USA, Inc.

Stelle, Ross (1995) *The French Way: Aspects of Behavior, Attitudes, and Customs of the French*. Lincolnwood, Illinois: Passport Books.

Taylor, Ally Adamson (1996) *Culture Shock! France*. Portland, Oregon: Graphic Arts Center Publishing.

Turkington, Carol (1999) *The Complete Idiot's Guide to Cultural Etiquette*. Indianapolis: Macmillan, USA.

REFERENCES

Agence France Presse (1991) "Not Where *They* Go When They Die," *International Herald Tribune*, October 30.

Alston, Jon P. (1990) *The Intelligent Businessman's Guide to Japan.* Tokyo, Japan: Charles E. Tuttle.

Bair, Deirdre (1990) *Simone de Beauvoir: A Biography.* New York: Summit.

Barsoux, Jean-Louis and Peter Lawrence (1990) M*anagement in France.* London: Cassell Educational.

Bernstein, Richard (1990) *Fragile Glory: A Portrait of France and the French.* New York: Knopf.

Blume, Mary (1999) *A French Affair: The Paris Beat.* New York: Free Press.

Bryant, Adam (1999) "Global Economics 101: What Is a C.E.O. Worth?" *The New York Times* January 17: A1, A4.

Carhart, Thad (2001) *The Piano Shop on the Left Bank: Discovering a Forgotten Passion in a Paris Atelier.* New York: Random House.

Carroll, Raymonde (1988) *Cultural Misunderstandings: The French-American Experience.* Chicago: University of Chicago Press.

Crozier, Michel (1964) *The Bureaucratic Phenomenon.* Chicago: University of Chicago Press.

_____ (1973) *The Stalled Society*. New York: Viking Press.

D'Iribarne, Philippe (1989) *La logique de l'honneur: Gestion des entreprises et traditions nationales*. Paris: Seuil.

Delaney, Kevin J. (1999) "Where the E in E-Shopping Stands for 'Extreme'," *The Wall Street Journal* October 14: B1, B17.

Elashmawi, Farid and Philip R. Harris (1993) *Multicultural Management: New Skills for Global Success*. Houston, USA: Gulf Publishing Company.

Fenby, Jonathan (1999) *France on the Brink*. New York: Arcade Publishing.

Foster, Dean Allen (1992) *Bargaining Across Borders: How to Negotiate Business Successfully Anywhere in the World*. New York: McGraw-Hill.

Goffman, Erving (1963) *Behavior in Public Places*. Glencoe, Illinois.: Free Press.

Gopnick, Adam (2000) *Paris to the Moon*. New York: Random House.

Gosset, Serge (1970) *Management: American and European Styles*. Belmont, CA: Wadsworth Publishing.

Graham, John (1996) "Vis-à-vis International Business Negotiations," Pp. 69-90 in Pervez N. Gauri and Jean-Claude Usinier (eds.) *International Business Negotiations*. New York: Pergamon.

Gordon, Colin (1996) *The Business Culture in France*. Oxford, England: Butterworth-Heinemann.

Hall, Edward T. and Mildred Reed Hall (1990) *Understanding Cultural Differences: Germans, French and Americans*. Yarmouth, Maine: Intercultural Press.

Hampden-Turner, Charles and Alfons Trompenaars (1993) *The Seven Cultures of Capitalism.* New York: Doubleday.

Hill, Richard (1994) *EuroManagers & Martians.* Brussels, Belgium: Europublications.

Hoffmann, Stanley (1977) "Entretien avec Stanley Hoffman," *Tel Quel* 71/72: 111-118.

Hofstede, Geert (1988) *Culture's Consequences: International Differences in Work-Related Values.* Beverly Hills, California: Sage.

Hofstede, Geert (1997) *Culture and Organizations: Software of the Mind.* New York: McGraw-Hill.

Inzerilli, Giorgio and André Laurent (1983) "Managerial Views of Organization Structure n France and the USA," *International Studies of Management and Organization* 13 (102): 97-118.

Landick, Marie (2000) "French Courts and Language Legislation," *French Cultural Studies* 31 (11-1): 131-148.

Laurent André (1983) "The Cultural Diversity of Western Conceptions of Management," *International Studies of Management and Organization* 13 (1-2): 75-96.

Lenski, Seymour Martin (1996) *American Exceptionalism: A Double-Edged Sword.* New York: Norton.

Levieux, Eleanor and Michel Levieux (1999) *Insiders' French.* Chicago: University of Chicago Press.

Lewis, Richard D. (2003) *The Cultural Imperative: Global Trends in the 21st Century.* Yarmouth, Maine: Intercultural Press.

Nora, Pierre (1998 [1977]) *Realms of Memory: The Construction of the French Past.* New York: Columbia University Press.

Oudot, Simone and David L. Gobert (1984) *La France: Culture, économie, commerce*. Boston: Houghton Mifflin.

Peyrefitte, Alain (1981 [1953]) *The Trouble with France*. New York: Knopf.

Platt, Polly (1995) *Friend or Foe? Getting the Most of Visiting, Living and Working in France*. Skokie, Illinois: Culture Crossings, Ltd.

_____ (2000) *Savoir Flair? 211 Tips for Enjoying France and the French*. London: Cultural Crossings, Ltd.

Pirouret, Roger (1968) *La France et le management*. Paris: Hommes et techniques et Editions Denoël.

Rabinow, Paul (1999) *French DNA: Trouble in Purgatory*. Chicago: University of Chicago Press.

Rochefort, Harriet Welty (1999) *French Toast: An American in Paris Celebrates the Maddening Mysteries of the French*. New York: St. Martin's.

Schneider, Susan C. and Jean-Louis Barsoux (2203) *Managing Across Cultures*. Harlow, England: Pearson Education Limited.

Trompenaars, Alfons (1993) *L'entreprise multi-culturelle*. Paris: Maxima.

_____ and Charles Hampden-Turner (1998) *Riding the Waves of Culture: Understanding Cultural Diversity in Global Business* (2nd ed.). New York: McGraw-Hill.

Woodruff, David (1999) "In France, Working Long Hours Becomes a Crime," *The Wall Street Journal* June 15: A15.

ABOUT THE AUTHORS

Jon P. Alston holds a doctorate in sociology from the University of Texas at Austin. He has taught in France and China, and has published six books, including *The Intelligent Businessman's Guide to Japan* and *Business Guide to Modern China*. He lives in College Station, Texas, where he has taught at Texas A&M University for 28 years.

Melanie Hawthorne is a professor of French at Texas A&M University. After taking a degree in French and philosophy at Oxford University, she worked briefly as an executive for an international market research company in London.

Sylvie Saillet has a Baccalauréate in economics and sociology, has worked for a number of business organizations, and is currently a student at the *École Supérieure de Commerce*, Dijon, France.

0-595-26462-X

Printed in the United States
55911LVS00004B/358

9 780595 264629